GO DO SOME GREAT THING

GO DO SOME GREAT THING

THE BLACK PIONEERS OF BRITISH COLUMBIA

CRAWFORD KILIAN

DOUGLAS & MCINTYRE
Vancouver

Douglas & McIntyre Ltd.
1875 Welch Street
North Vancouver, B.C.

Canadian Cataloguing in Publication Data

Kilian, Crawford, 1941–
    Go do some great thing

    Bibliography: p. 173
    Includes index.
    ISBN 0–88894–180–3

    1. Blacks–British Columbia–History.
I. Title.
FC3850.N3K5   971.1'004'96   C78–002008–1
F1089.7.N3K5

Cover design by Nancy Legue-Grout
Typesetting by The Typeworks, Mayne Island, British Columbia
Printed and bound in Canada by The Hunter Rose Company

This book is dedicated to the memory of
all of Canada's Black pioneers,
to their descendants,
and to Ervin R. Wilkerson —
a good boss, a good friend, a comrade in arms.

CONTENTS

PHOTOGRAPHIC
ACKNOWLEDGMENTS

The following photographs are reproduced here with the permission of the Provincial Archives, Victoria:

Mifflin Wistar Gibbs
Sir James Douglas
Amor De Cosmos
Sir Matthew Baillie Begbie
The sugar sculpture ridiculing the delegates
    to the Yale Convention
Peter Lester
Mrs. Peter Lester
Samuel Booth
Robert Clanton
Victoria Richard Clanton
James Barnswell
Mary Lowe Barnswell
The "African Rifles"
Fielding William Spotts
Fielding Spotts, Jr.
Charles and Nancy Alexander
Sylvia Stark
Willis Stark and Jim Anderson
Mrs. John T. Pierre
Richard Stokes

The Vancouver City Archives provided the following photographs:

Philip Sullivan
Josephine Sullivan
Seraphim ("Joe") Fortes

INTRODUCTION

L ike most British Columbians, I learned only by chance that Black people had been living in the province since the gold rush of 1858. Surprised and interested, I pursued the subject. There were few references to the Black pioneers in most historical studies, and — though I did not know it yet — some writers had distorted the facts.

As my research became more systematic, I found some reliable modern sources, most notably James W. Pilton's M.A. thesis, completed at the University of British Columbia in 1951; these sources led me in turn to the documents and newspaper accounts that first recorded the Blacks' arrival and early struggles. It was a vivid, dramatic, often violent story, told with the most eloquence by some of the Blacks themselves. In their new home, the pioneers had contended with bigotry, political chicanery, epidemics, and even murder — as well as the normal hazards and hardships of frontier life.

I soon came to respect the Blacks' courage and resourcefulness in the face of these obstacles; I also wondered why scarcely anyone seemed interested in their experience. Information was available only in fragments. Pilton's thesis was unpublished. British Columbia's scholarly journals printed an occasional article on some aspect of the pioneers' story; somewhat less accurately, so did popular magazines and newspapers. In regional histories of such places as Saltspring Island, Kamloops, and the Peace River country, mention was made in passing of Black pioneers such as the Starks, John Freemont Smith, and Daniel Williams. With few exceptions, these accounts treated such individuals as curiosities, mere anecdotes in the province's "real" history; when not romanticizing or patronizing the Blacks, they often betrayed outright racism. Even historians sometimes took as fact the bigoted opinions of the Blacks' white contemporaries.

In effect, then, the Black pioneers of British Columbia had become what Orwell called "unpersons." They had played a key role in the early years of the colonies that became British Columbia, and yet the province had forgotten them. Fools, knaves, and madmen have given their names to British Columbia's streets and towns; the only monument to the Blacks is a drinking fountain dedicated to Joe Fortes, the lifeguard of English Bay beach.

No doubt the chief reward of any life is the living of it, but it seemed to me that the Black pioneers deserved far more recognition than a handful of newspaper features, a couple of place names, and a drinking fountain. So, though not a trained historian, I decided to write their story myself.

In a book intended for nonspecialist readers, I have tried to identify my sources without resorting to footnotes. Those familiar with James Pilton's thesis will recognize how much I owe to his research. Later work has added to it, but has changed few of his findings. Pilton led me in turn to many original sources: newspapers, unpublished memoirs, and contemporary accounts such as the books by Lt. R.M. Mayne and Rev. Matthew Macfie. The staff of the Provincial Archives in Victoria gave me invaluable assistance, as did the staff of the Capilano College Library, the University of B.C. Library, the Vancouver Public Library, and the Vancouver City Archives. W.E. Bigglestone, archivist of Oberlin College in Ohio, supplied a great deal of information about several Black pioneers who were alumni of that college; John L. Ferguson of the Arkansas Historical Commission provided a wealth of information on the later years of Mifflin Gibbs. News features by Alan Morley, James K. Nesbitt, and Paul St. Pierre provided both useful information and valuable leads to new sources.

A great many individuals offered information and encouragement without which this book could never have been completed. These include Chester Alexander, Harold Alexander, Mary

Alexander, Norman Alexander, and Verna Alexander; Emery Barnes, MLA; Earl Barnswell; Leon Bibb; John Braithwaite; Rosemary Brown, MLA; Bob Chaplin; Jesse Dillard; Irene Duncan; Ruth Ford; Don Fraser; Myrtle Holloman; Cam Hubert; E.J. Image; Edward Meade; Art Sherman; Rudy Spence; Nan E. Tremayne; Peggy C. Walker; R. Whims; Ernie Wilby; Paul Winn, and Tom Wylie. The late Jack Wasserman deserves a special note of thanks for his help; British Columbians of all races lost a friend and advocate at his untimely death. Thanks should also go to the many people who wrote me to express their interest in the book.

The last word on any subject is an epitaph, and the Blacks of British Columbia are still very much alive. I hope that this book, as an informal and incomplete history, will encourage professional historians to re-examine the role of the Blacks in the province, past and present, and to fill in the gaps and correct the errors of fact and interpretation which this book no doubt contains. Until that much-needed work is done, I hope this book will help to remind all British Columbians of how much we owe the Blacks, and to give them a fresh appreciation of the contributions which all our racial minorities have made to our common welfare.

CHAPTER ONE

"Free negroes and other obnoxious persons"

O ne day in the early 1850s, a well known customer entered the Clay Street boot shop run by Peter Lester and Mifflin Wistar Gibbs, two of San Francisco's most successful Black merchants. After examining a pair of boots, the customer asked Lester to set them aside for awhile, saying he wanted to think about buying them. The proprietors were glad to oblige. A few minutes later another white man, a friend of the first, came in and tried the same boots on. He insisted on buying them. When Lester and Gibbs tried to explain that the boots were being kept for his friend, the man assured them that he would personally explain the matter; then he left the store.

Very shortly afterward, the two merchants found that a brutal kind of joke was being played on them. Both white men entered the store. The first one pretended to be furious over the sale of the boots, and swore viciously at Lester. While the Black men tried to explain, the first customer struck savagely at Lester with his cane. Neither Lester nor Gibbs dared to resist; both whites were armed, and there was no one else in the store. After beating Lester bloody, the white men left, serene in the knowledge that their victim had no hope of redress: under California law, no Black could testify in court against a white man.

In a gold-rush town where murder was commonplace, the incident might have seemed trivial, a normal hazard of doing business. Added to many similar incidents, however, the beating helped to start one of the most remarkable yet little-known mass migrations in the history of North America. After a decade of beatings, insults, and legalized injustice, some six hundred Black Californians would emigrate north to the British colony of Vancouver Island, and to the gold fields of the mainland of what is now British Columbia, Canada's westernmost province. Their story was to be one of triumph and betrayal, of bitter humiliation and quiet success. The Blacks would affect the course of Canadian history; in fact, by helping to preserve British Columbia, they helped to ensure that Canada itself would maintain its independence of the United States. The Blacks' experience in the rough, rich, bizarre Northwest would foreshadow that of later immigrants, including the war resisters and deserters of the 1960s. And while the Blacks were to be used as political pawns by some of British Columbia's rulers, some of them in turn would use B.C. as a stepping-stone to greater things.

As Lester and Gibbs cleaned themselves up in their disordered shop, however, they were not yet thinking of escape. Intelligent, educated, and idealistic, they were already—in their early thirties— veterans of the struggle of abolish slavery and improve the status of free Blacks in the United States. Gibbs, in particular, had been active since his youth in Philadelphia, where he had been born and raised. He had worked for the Philadelphia "station" of the underground railway, helping escaped slaves travel north to freedom in Canada. At the age of 22, he had been part of a delegation to petition the Pennsylvania state government for Black enfranchisement. At 25, he had spoken publicly at a rally held to honor Louis Kossuth, the Hungarian liberator—a rally to which Blacks had not been invited. A year later, in 1849, he had traveled through New York State with Frederick Douglass, speaking against slavery to often hostile audiences.

At the end of the tour, disheartened and with no real sense of achievement, Gibbs got some advice from Julia Griffith, a Black abolitionist: "What! discouraged? Go do some great thing." He did. On borrowed money, Gibbs had traveled steerage class to San Francisco, where he had worked at everything from carpentry to shining shoes. At length he had gone into partnership with Lester, and their business had flourished.

Gibbs had not left his political activism behind him in Philadelphia. In 1851, he was one of a group of Blacks who published a protest against their lack of the vote — a protest that startled many complacent white Californians. In the mid-'50s, Gibbs took a major part in the Black conventions which met repeatedly to draft memorials to be sent to the state legislature in Sacramento. He was also one of the publishers of California's first Black newspaper, *The Mirror of the Times.*

While his work for the underground railway was technically illegal, Gibbs clearly preferred to work within the system — to win under white rules by patient agitation and economic success. At the end of his long career, he was to advise young Blacks to "Labor to make yourself as indispensable as possible in all your relations with the dominant race, and color will cut less and less figure in your upward grade." Good advice, no doubt, but in the 1850s Gibbs witnessed a concerted effort to make California's Blacks as dispensable as possible — to solve the "Negro question" by driving the Blacks out of the state.

Anti-Black feeling had existed in California since the gold rush. Almost as soon as it came into existence, the state legislature, in its 1850 Civil Practice Act, had disqualified Blacks from testifying against whites. When, in 1853, a memorial was presented to the legislature asking for repeal of that provision, one of the assembly-men suggested, amid much hilarity, that the request be thrown out the window. His motion was carried unanimously.

Such an attitude was predictable in a state with a sizable minority of white southerners and with a government dominated by Democrats sympathetic to the south. In criticizing the law disqualifying Blacks from testifying, a San Francisco newspaper editorialized in 1857: "It is maintained in force simply because a class of our people were brought up in states where negroes were not allowed to testify, not because they were negroes, but because they were slaves, and their vehement adherence to the prejudices of their birthplace has infected the popular mind."

The state legislature did not stop with one law. A Fugitive Slave Act was passed in 1852; this act permitted the arrest of any escaped slave found in the state, and his return to servitude provided that he was taken out of California. As if the Civil Practice Act were not enough, the 1852 law specified that "In no trial or hearing under this Act shall the testimony of such alleged fugitive be admitted in evidence."

The Act had been used almost at once against three slaves owned by a Georgian named Perkins, who had had them arrested and transported back to the south. The slaves were unable to testify that Perkins had promised them their freedom when he had brought them into the state in 1849, and had allowed them to work to save money to buy themselves out of slavery. Although the Act lapsed in 1855, southerners still brought "indentured servants" into California. These were invariably Black; if they were hired out to other employers, their masters collected their wages. Since no slaves escaped from the south seeking freedom in California, the effect of the Act was to make life easy for slaveholders. They could bring their slaves in as "servants," exploit them as slaves, and — when they were ready to return to the south — declare their servants to be fugitive slaves in fact.

Blacks whose freedom was unquestioned also faced legalized injustice. In San Francisco, they owned five million dollars' worth of property, and were taxed accordingly; they also paid a poll tax. But when they tried to vote, they were driven from the polls. Mifflin Gibbs and Peter Lester protested this unfairness by refusing to pay the poll tax in 1857. Their goods were promptly seized and put up for auction to pay the tax. However, a sympathetic white southerner persuaded the other people at the auction to "give the goods a severe letting alone." Since no one bid on them, the goods were returned; thereafter, the poll tax was no longer enforced.

Peter Lester's family also faced discrimination when the San Francisco public schools were segregated in January of 1858 and his daughter Sarah was expelled from the school she had been attending. A minority on the school board argued that an exception should be made for her, since she was no darker than her classmates.

The problem, as the Blacks realized, was not really the southerners in the state; it was the northern white majority, who detested all Blacks, free or slave. Their point of view was expressed in an 1857 newspaper editorial praising Oregon's new constitution because it expressly forbade free Blacks from entering the state: "It is much better to keep them away than to let them come, and deprive them of all civil rights and the power of defending themselves, as is done in this state."

California's dubious status as a free state was further undermined when John B. Weller was inaugurated as governor in January 1858. In his first public statement, Weller straddled the fence on the national issue of slavery. California had chosen to forbid it, he observed, but to attack slavery elsewhere in the Union was unwise, since it amounted to meddling in other states' internal affairs, and would "weaken the ties of affection between the States." Such hypocrisy was typical of the attitudes that led within a few weeks to a crisis which nearly took California into the pro-slavery camp and which led directly to the Black emigration to the Northwest.

The issue was the fate of Archy Lee, a "fugitive slave" of 19 who in January of 1858 was being held for deportation. His owner, a young Mississippian named Charles A. Stovall, claimed to be traveling for his health through the state, not residing there permanently. Archy, his slave for many years and valued at $1,500, had accompanied him on the western journey as Stovall's manservant. For a transient, Stovall had made himself very much at home in California. He had "traveled for his health" with a herd of cattle, which he placed on a ranch he purchased in the Carson Valley. He had hired a schoolroom in Sacramento and advertised for pupils, and had put Archy out to work while collecting his wages.

The U.S. commissioner who heard the case ruled that Archy was not a fugitive slave and therefore could not be deported, but the commissioner declined to decide what should be done with him, and turned the case over to the state court.

Abolitionists and supporters of slavery followed the case closely, and each side gave what help it could. The Blacks of San Francisco raised money for Archy's defense, while Stovall's friends in the state legislature tried to strengthen the southerner's cause. On January 18, just a week after the case had become public knowledge, Assemblyman A.G. Stokes introduced a bill providing that when a slave "shall be brought or *may have been heretofore brought*" into California by an owner only traveling through — or briefly sojourning — the owner should have his property restored to him if the slave attempted escape. This bill would not merely have given Stovall legal grounds for regaining possession of Archy, it would have legalized slavery in California. Stokes went on, a few weeks later, to frame another bill "to prohibit the immigration of free negroes and other obnoxious persons into this state and to protect and regulate the conduct of such persons now within the state."

The political atmosphere surrounding the case grew still more acrid in February, when the state Supreme Court handed down its decision — a decision which at once took its place as one of the most astounding judicial farces in American history. Chief Justice Terry and Judge Burnett ruled that Stovall was *not* visiting or traveling in California, and was therefore a resident of a free state who was trying to uphold slavery in that state. But, since Stovall was ill, insolvent, and young, and this was the first such case to arise in California, they continued, "We are not disposed to rigidly enforce the rule for the first time. But in reference to all future cases it is our purpose to enforce the rules strictly according to their true intent and spirit."

A later Supreme Court judge, in commenting on this decision, observed that it "gave the law to the north and the nigger to the south." He added that Terry and Burnett had in effect declared that the Constitution did not apply to young men traveling for their health; that it did not apply the first time; and that Supreme Court decisions were not to be taken as precedents. The court's decision was also met with an eruption of outrage from Blacks and abolitionists.

Stovall, however, had Archy. Seeing that California was no longer a very good place for his health, he arranged to sail for Panama on the steamer *Orizaba* on March 4. Until then, he kept Archy secretly locked up in the San Joaquin county jail. The Blacks discovered Archy's whereabouts and applied for a writ of *habeas corpus* to gain his release. Stovall evaded being served with this writ, and hid Archy elsewhere. Undiscouraged, the Blacks made plans for a dramatic last-minute rescue.

The *Orizaba* left San Francisco as scheduled on March 4; Stovall and Archy were not aboard. As the steamer approached the Golden Gate, however, a small boat carrying the two men put out from shore and came alongside. Thinking he had successfully outwitted his enemies, Stovall was chagrined to find policemen on board with a warrant for his arrest on a charge of kidnapping. Furious, he drew a pistol, but was quickly disarmed by the police after a spirited scuffle. "The Supreme Court gave me this boy," he shouted, "and I'll be damned if any other court in this state will take him away."

The police took Stovall and Archy off the steamer and rowed back to a city shivering with tension. A large crowd of Blacks had gathered on the docks to welcome Archy back, but they were far from overjoyed; news had just reached them that the state Senate judicial committee in Sacramento had recommended continuance of the prohibition against Black testimony. Archy's oppressor might well escape punishment, thanks to that law.

On Friday, March 5, a mass meeting was held in the Zion Methodist Episcopal Church at Pacific and Stockton to support Archy's cause. A large, predominantly Black crowd contributed $150 to Archy's legal costs, and set up a committee to raise more. This was to be the first in a series of meetings, and their purpose would advance from saving one Black to saving the whole community.

The following Monday, in a packed courtroom, Judge Freelon turned down Stovall's application to dismiss the writ of *habeas corpus;* Stovall's lawyer, seeing nothing else to do, consented to Archy's being granted his freedom. The crowd was then astounded to see Archy immediately arrested as a fugitive slave, and ordered back to jail. A near-riot broke out, and the U.S. Marshal charged with escorting Archy to jail had to call for reinforcements before he could get the boy out of the courtroom. Archy was dragged through the streets at the head of an angry procession of Blacks and sympathetic whites; several Black men were arrested for assault and battery before Archy was behind bars again.

To the Blacks of San Francisco, this stunning development must have seemed like proof that the law was a grotesquely flexible set of rules designed to keep them in bondage, but they fought stubbornly on in the courts. Their trust in the law must have been further shaken on March 19, when Bill 339 was introduced in the legislature by J.S. Warfield: "An Act to restrict and prevent the immigration to and residence in the State of negroes and mulattoes."

Obviously intended as an improvement on Stokes's earlier efforts, Bill 339 was grossly racist. Under its provisions, no Black would henceforth be allowed to immigrate to California; those who did would be deported at their own expense, for the state would be empowered to hire them out to anyone "for such reasonable time as shall be necessary to pay the costs of the conviction and transportation from this state before sending such negro or mulatto therefrom." Blacks already residing in the state would be required to register; failure to do so would be a misdemeanor. Every registered Black would have to be licensed to work, and anyone employing an unlicensed Black would be heavily fined. Probably the cruelest provision of the bill would have made it a misdemeanor to bring a slave into California with the intent of freeing him. This provision was aimed at Blacks who, having bought their own freedom and earned enough money, wished to buy the freedom of their own families still in the slave states.

The effect of Bill 339 would have been to legalize slavery in California as long as the government itself was the slaveholder. There was considerable support for the bill—we are all socialists when the government does what we want it to—but also some sharp criticism of it. One of the best rebukes to Warfield's proposed law came from Mifflin Gibbs in a letter to the San Francisco *Daily Evening Bulletin:* "Let the bill now before the Legislature take what turn it may, the colored people in this state have no regrets to offer for their deportment. *Their* course has been manly, industrious, law-abiding. To this Legislature and the press that sustains them be all the honor, glory and consequences of prosecuting and abusing an industrious, unoffending and defenceless people."

The case of Archy Lee now took another bizarre turn. Stovall made a new affidavit in an attempt to make Archy seem to be a fugitive slave. Stovall now claimed that Archy had assaulted someone in Mississippi in January 1857, and had then fled west. Stovall, traveling west a little later, had encountered Archy by chance on the North Platte River and traveled to Sacramento with him. Obviously, Stovall was relying on the Civil Practice Act to keep Archy from disproving this new story; he was also relying on either stupidity or blind partisanship in the U.S. commissioner, George Pen Johnston, a Democrat who heard the case. Johnston, politically sympathetic but no fool, ruled that Archy was not a fugitive slave, and granted him his freedom on April 14.

Though delighted with the decision, the Blacks did not deceive themselves that a new era of racial justice was at hand. Bill 339 was still moving through the legislature to what seemed inevitable enactment. (It did not, in fact, become law, but only because last-minute amendments prevented its coming to a vote before the legislature adjourned.) All the other repressive laws were still on the books, and California was still a violent state where many disputes were settled with a gun; indeed, Commissioner Johnston himself was to kill a man in a duel before the end of the summer.

Those Blacks who had sweated to earn money or property saw little chance of holding what they had gained; those who had yet to succeed saw little chance of doing so. They were a tiny minority, an estimated four thousand out of the state's half-million. California was an El Dorado for white men only.

On the evening of April 14, a mass meeting was held again at Zion Church, partly to raise an additional $400 for Archy's legal costs but chiefly to discuss possible destinations for a mass emigration of the Black community.

The meeting opened with a hymn entitled "The Year of Archy Lee," composed for the occasion:

> Blow ye the trumpet! Blow!
> The gladly solemn sound,
> Let all the nations know
> To earth's remotest bound
> The year of Archy Lee is come,
> Return, ye ransomed Stovall, home.
>
> Exalt the Lamb of God!
> The sin-atoning Lamb;
> Redemption for His blood
> Through all the land proclaim.
> The year of Archy Lee is come,
> Return, ye ransomed Stovall, home.
>
> Ye slaves of sin and hell,
> Your liberty receive;
> And safe in Jesus dwell,
> And blest in Jesus live.
> The year of Archy Lee is come,
> Return, ye ransomed Stovall, home.
>
> The gospel trumpet hear
> The news of pardoning grace;
> Ye happy should draw near
> Behold your Saviour's face.
> The year of Archy Lee is come,
> Return, ye ransomed Stovall, home.

Another song was also sung to celebrate the liberation of Archy

Lee. It was called "A Song of Praise." and was subtitled "For the Benefit of Those Named Therein."

Sound the glad tidings o'er land and o'er sea —
Our people have triumphed and Archy is free!
Sing, for the pride of the tyrant is broken,
The decision of Burnett and Terry reversed.
How vain was their boasting! Their plans so soon broken;
Archy's free and Stovall is brought to the dust.
Praise to the Judges and praise to the lawyers!
Freedom was their object and that they obtained.
Stovall was shown it was time to be moving;
He left on the steamer to lay deeper plans.
But there was a Baker, a Crosby, and Tompkins,
Before Pen Johnston and did plead for the man.

After Archy himself was presented to the cheering crowd of five hundred, the meeting turned to discussion of emigration. Three possibilities presented themselves: Panama, the Mexican state of Sonora, and the British colony of Vancouver Island. Since most of the Blacks had seen enough of Panama en route to California, there was little interest in this choice, though an inquiry was sent to General Bosques, president of the Panamanian Senate (his very favorable reply arrived in July, when the Blacks were committed to Vancouver Island). One man at the meeting argued strongly for Sonora as a better site for an agricultural settlement, but could arouse little interest; Sonora, just south of the Arizona Territory, had already suffered several "filibusters" — raids by Americans seeking to annex it to the United States — and it seemed certain to become U.S. territory before long.

Interest in Vancouver Island was heightened by the appearance at the meeting of Jeremiah Nagle, captain of the steamer *Commodore,* which was on the San Francisco-Victoria run. Standing by the pulpit with maps of Vancouver Island, Nagle answered a rapid stream of questions about the colony. He also had with him a letter from "a gentleman in the service of the Hudson's Bay Company of undoubted veracity," giving details about the colony and welcoming the Blacks. This gentleman must have been the governor himself, James Douglas.

In reporting on the meeting, the *Daily Evening Bulletin* predicted that the emigration would come to nothing, but the paper was proven wrong in less than a week. On April 19, another meeting was held to form a "Pioneer Committee" of sixty-five Blacks who were to embark next day on the *Commodore* for Victoria. In the event, only thirty-five were able to clear up their affairs in time, but the next day they were seen off by almost the entire Black community at the Pacific and Folsom Street wharves.

It was a noisy, confused afternoon. In addition to the *Commodore,* two other vessels — the *Golden Age* and the *Columbia* — were also leaving for the north; each had a "barker" extolling the advantages of his own ship. Fruit vendors and newsboys wandered through the crowds. Mifflin Gibbs gave a farewell address to the Pioneer Committee, but no one paid much attention. The reason for the uproar was simple enough. Nagle had also brought confirmation of the rumors that had been filtering down from the Northwest: there was gold on the Fraser and Thompson Rivers in the British territory of New Caledonia. And Victoria was the gateway to the gold fields.

As the *Commodore* steamed out of San Francisco on that late spring afternoon, the Blacks of the Pioneer Committee must have felt mixed emotions. Ahead was a land that seemed to offer equality, opportunity, and perhaps even great wealth. But the four hundred white men who were their fellow-passengers must have looked grimly familiar.

CHAPTER TWO

"I think the land is full of gold."

The land to which the Black Californians had been invited was one of the last parts of North America to feel the impact of European expansion, and until 1858 that impact had been relatively light. Lying north of the Columbia River, west of the Rocky Mountains, and south of Alaska, the Pacific Northwest was at the farthest extent of four empires: Russia, Spain, Britain, and the young United States. By the end of the eighteenth century, Russia was content with Alaska; Spain had withdrawn to California, leaving Britain in possession. The British, however, were soon obliged to share part of the Northwest with the United States. During the first half of the nineteenth century, the remoteness of the region and the lack of settlers kept the two powers from conflict over the Northwest, although both sides expected an eventual confrontation for mastery.

But the Northwest was little known, and explorers' reports portrayed it as grim and uninviting. The interior was a labyrinth of mountains and rivers, sparsely inhabited by warlike Indians. The westernmost of the mountain ranges plunged steeply into the sea, creating 17,000 miles of shoreline in the 500 miles between Puget Sound and Alaska. Dark, dense forests of hemlock, cedar and fir mantled the mountains right down to tidewater, interrupted only by steep rivers falling violently into countless fjords and inlets. Captain George Vancouver, who mapped much of this coast in 1792, found it beautiful but depressing. Describing the coast near the site of the city that would one day bear his name, he wrote:

"The low fertile shore we had been accustomed to see, though lately with some interruptions, here no longer existed; their place was now occupied by the base of the stupendous snowy barrier [the Coast Range], thinly wooded, and rising from the sea abruptly to the clouds; from whose frigid summit, the dissolving snow in foaming torrents rushed down the sides and chasms of its rugged surface, exhibiting altogether a sublime, though gloomy spectacle, which animated nature seemed to have deserted."

Barrenness was a mistaken impression. The coastline teemed with life. The rivers and sea were filled with millions of salmon, halibut, cod and other fish; the schools of herring were so dense that they could be literally raked from the water. Traders from England, Russia, and the U.S. were already hunting sea otters, whose furs brought high prices in China. Shellfish crusted the rocky shores, and the forests were full of deer, edible plants, and berries.

This abundance of food had for centuries supported one of the largest native populations anywhere in North America. As Vancouver himself learned, the Indians of the Northwest Coast had developed complex societies, with technologies advanced enough to make good use of the country's resources. The Haida of the Queen Charlotte Islands, for example, built ocean-going canoes in which they hunted whales and ventured as far as California to trade and raid. It is possible that they even traveled as far as Japan. While the Indians' metallurgy was chiefly limited to copper, they were familiar with iron — obtained either through trade with Asia or by salvage of shipwrecked Japanese vessels — and they were master craftsmen in wood.

Vancouver found in the Indians "an ardent desire for commercial transactions," and his arrival marked the beginning of a long period of commerce that was to make the development of the Northwest radically different from that of other American frontiers. Too remote to be worth conquering, too sophisticated to be easily demoralized by European culture, the Northwest Indians used trade to develop their own culture to a remarkable level.

This culture was already, in many respects, the most advanced one north of Mexico. When Vancouver arrived, the natural wealth of food and timber was supporting a population estimated by Wilson Duff at 86,000 — one third of the total native population of

British America. Two or three months' easy work produced enough
food — salmon, venison, roots and berries — to sustain a family all
year. What was not locally available could be traded for, either
up and down the coast or in the interior. As a result, the Indians
faced the same problem the whites would later encounter: what
to do with all their wealth.

Given a high standard of living and plenty of leisure, the Indians
became renowned artists and craftsmen. Their societies were
rigidly stratified, but one could rise in power and status by "pot-
latching" — ceremonially giving away huge amounts of goods.
Even women could and did rise to the status of chief by this method.
Ambition was thus satisfied, wealth was distributed, and work
was created for traders and craftsmen. European trade increased
the wealth, permitting — indeed, demanding — even greater dis-
plays of opulence.

War was another leisure activity which trade enhanced. The
chief purposes of warfare were to gain booty and slaves, though
territorial expansion was sometimes a motive. The booty was to
be given away; the slaves were mostly for show, since only a rich
man could afford to keep involuntary dependents who did little
work.

For more than a generation, therefore, trade with Europe enabled the northwest coast Indians to work out the logical consequences of their own cultural values. But even as iron tools permitted them to carve ever-larger totem poles, and as firearms enhanced their warlike ambitions, the coast peoples entered a dark
age from which they are only now, over a century later, beginning
to emerge. They were growing too dependent on guns, iron, alcohol, and other white trade goods; disease, drink, and increased
tribal warfare decimated them even as their culture reached its
zenith. Unlike their neighbors in Oregon and California, however,
the Indians did not collapse under the weight of growing numbers
of white settlers. The Northwest was for a long time thinly peopled
by Europeans as a direct result of the policies of the gigantic enterprise known as the Hudson's Bay Company.

The HBC had enjoyed a trade monopoly since 1670 over a region
known as Rupert's Land — a vaguely defined wilderness including most of what is now Canada west of Lake Superior and east
of the Rockies. In 1821, the British government granted the com-

pany the right to trade west of the Rockies in two districts: New Caledonia in the north and Columbia in the south. In effect, a vast portion of North America became the private property of a single corporation. The American West was conquered largely by adventurers, entrepreneurs, and pioneers whose individualism took it close to anarchy. The Northwest, by contrast, was run by clerks — organization men in an almost military hierarchy, working for a corporate employer in London.

Company traders had no desire to exterminate the Indians, who after all were the company's chief suppliers of furs and its chief customers for trade goods. The HBC made a policy of supplying first-rate merchandise in exchange for furs, and where it had a monopoly it refused to sell liquor; the traders knew that alcohol was bad for business. Neither did the company want to encourage white settlement. Settlers would bring an inevitable challenge to the company's monopoly and its eventual displacement as the government of the region. For years, therefore, the only whites living permanently in the Northwest were HBC employees.

What the company wanted was not what it had to settle for. American expansion into the Columbia district was rapid, and from the standpoint of the British and Indians, the quality of these newcomers was alarming: "worthless and lawless characters," one Englishman called them. In Oregon, the southern part of Columbia district, the Americans quickly formed a provisional government (excluding the French-Canadian settlers on the Columbia River), appealed for U.S. annexation, and talked seriously of driving out of the country any white with an Indian wife. By international treaty, Englishmen and Americans were guaranteed equal access to the Columbia district, so the HBC could do nothing to hinder the newcomers. Surviving largely thanks to the HBC's generous credit and assistance, the Americans ungratefully threatened to storm and loot its supplies at Fort Vancouver, across the Columbia from modern Portland, Oregon. To the HBC traders, the Americans must have seemed very much like those who had taken Texas from the Mexicans a decade or so earlier.

In 1846, the boundary between British and American territory was set at the 49th parallel. But the few hundred British subjects north of the line saw that there was no real obstacle to an American takeover right up to 54° 40" — the border of Russian Alaska. If

Britain were to hold the Northwest, some kind of political entity had to be created. Reluctantly, the company agreed to establish a Crown Colony on Vancouver Island in 1850. It did so, however, on its own terms. Virtually every white man in the new colony was a company employee and did as the company ordered. The first governor, Richard Blanshard, came out from England ill-prepared to deal with the situation, and soon found he could do nothing unless his action suited the company. He quit in less than a year. London was obliged to appoint as the next governor the man who had already been the *de facto* ruler of the Northwest for years: James Douglas, the company's Chief Factor on the coast.

There was probably no one in the British Empire better qualified for the job. Douglas's knowledge of the country was based on 25 years' experience; his administrative skills were great; even his pomposity, arrogance, and autocratic style of government were assets in dealing with Indians and whites alike. Had anyone else attempted to govern the new colony during the 1850s and early 1860s, it is likely that British Columbia—perhaps all of western Canada—would have become part of the United States.

James Douglas was born in Demerara, British Guiana, in 1803. His father was a Glasgow-born merchant who had settled in Demerara to run the family's sugar plantations. Little is known of James Douglas's mother except that she was a Creole, probably of mixed Black and white ancestry. Though Douglas and his brother and sister were illegitimate, their father recognized them as his, and provided for their upbringing after he left the country and married a Scotswoman. Douglas was sent to school in Scotland, and after a solid education he sailed to Canada in 1819 as a clerk for the North West Company—fur traders in competition with the Hudson's Bay Company. Within a year he was actively involved in the fierce rivalry between the Nor'Westers and the HBC along the Churchill River in what is now northern Saskatchewan. Tall, rugged, and muscular, he was physically and temperamentally suited to a hard country. The circumstances of his birth were no disadvantage; the fur traders were interested in profits, not their employees' backgrounds. Both companies were colorblind, and had often employed Blacks, Indians, and Metis of French-Indian ancestry. Douglas's brother was fired from the Nor'Westers for "stupidity" while Douglas himself rose fairly rapidly. He transferred to the HBC when it absorbed the Nor'Westers in 1821. In 1825 he was sent across the Rockies to Fort St. James, in New Caledonia, where he soon married the half-breed daughter of the Chief Factor.

While much of his work was no doubt unexciting and routine, Douglas showed that he could think fast and act decisively. The company made and enforced all the law there was in New Caledonia, and when the young clerk learned that an Indian murderer was hiding in a nearby village, he is said to have entered the village and dragged the man out by the hair. According to one version of the story, Douglas personally blew the man's brains out; other accounts state that he allowed his assistants to execute the criminal. But he had a nice talent for frontier diplomacy as well: once, when a local band of Indians was angered about some minor incident, Douglas smoothed things over by issuing large amounts of biscuits and molasses. "Dear me, dear me," he murmered as the feasting Indians forgot their grievance, "what a lot of good a little molasses can do!"

In 1830, Douglas was transferred south to Fort Vancouver, where he was to spend the next twenty years. He was already seen by his superiors as a likely man to rise in the company, although he encountered snubs from proper Englishmen who disapproved of his marriage "according to the custom of the country" to a half-Indian. James and Amelia Douglas were not formally married until 1837.

Of more concern to Douglas, however, was the growing pressure of the Americans; by the end of the 1830s, it was clear that they would eventually displace the British from the Columbia district, despite Britain's superior claim to the territory. In the early 1840s, Douglas—now a Chief Factor—recommended that the company move its headquarters to the southern tip of Vancouver Island. In 1843, he personally supervised the building of Fort Victoria; six years later, after the Columbia district was relinquished to the United States, the new fort did become the HBC headquarters on the coast. A year later, Victoria was also the capital of the new Crown Colony.

When Douglas became its second governor, in 1851, the colony's prospects were poor. Under the terms laid down by London, the company had to charge one pound sterling per acre to prospective settlers, who in turn had to guarantee to put a certain number of people on the land. This was a strong discouragement to growth, since anyone could obtain 640 acres in Washington Territory for nothing and since land in Oregon was only a few cents per acre. In addition, the Crown recognized the Indians' possession of the land, and Douglas was obliged to buy it from them before he could sell it to Europeans. While the Indians would accept very little (most of Victoria's townsite was purchased from the Songhees for "371 blankets and a cap"), Douglas had very little money available for buying land. So, although the Indians were eager to sell and at least a few settlers were eager to buy, growth was stymied by the poverty of the government.

As long as population growth was slow, Douglas did not feel much pressure to carry out London's terms for establishing political institutions in the colony. The government was supposed to consist of a governor, an appointed council, and an elected assembly. Governor Blanshard had appointed the council—Douglas and two others—before he left, but his successor preferred to run things without often consulting the council. The lack of settlers permitted him to postpone creation of the elected assembly until 1856, when he was ordered to do so by the Colonial Office. Totally opposed to universal suffrage, and unfamiliar with democratic institutions, Douglas set stiff property qualifications for voters and candidates. No one could vote for an assemblyman without owning at least 20 acres of land, or run for a seat without "300 pounds sterling worth of freehold property or immoveable estate." In the three electoral districts outside Victoria Town, this meant that candidates took their seats unopposed, and in Victoria itself the election of 1856 was decided by a handful of votes.

In the early years of his administration, therefore, Douglas ruled as an autocrat, and had to deal single-handedly with events. One of his first challenges came in 1851, when gold was discovered in the Queen Charlotte Islands, off the northern mainland coast. Miners from California swarmed to the islands, and Douglas— though he had no legal right to do so—asserted the rights of the Crown over the islands' new inhabitants. London belatedly supported his measures.

Though the American presence in the Queen Charlottes was transient, Douglas had seen—as he had on the Columbia—how quickly his southern neighbors could occupy any part of the northwest coast. A few years later he was faced with a similar, but far more serious, predicament.

In 1855, a few American prospectors began working their way up the Columbia into British territory. The following year they found gold, though in small amounts, and still more miners filtered across the border. When they moved on to the Fraser and Thompson Rivers, they began to find real paydirt. Rumors of the strikes soon reached Douglas in Victoria, along with samples of ore, but word did not stop there. By March of 1858, the American settlements on Puget Sound were deserted after reports reached them that miners were making up to fifty dollars a day from the Fraser's gold-rich sand bars. This time, Douglas was convinced that a real rush would soon be underway. As he himself told one group of miners a few months later, "I think that the country is full of gold, and that east and north and south of Fraser's River there is a gold-field of incalculable extent."

Douglas knew that the news would reach San Francisco within days and would lure huge numbers of Americans into Victoria en route to the mouth of the Fraser, across Georgia Strait. Many would stop in Victoria; others would settle down on the mainland, where the HBC was still the only form of authority. Late in 1857, he had — quite illegally — proclaimed Crown ownership of all mines on the mainland, and required prospectors to pay 21 shillings (about $5) "to dig, search for, and remove gold." As in the case of the Queen Charlottes, the Colonial Office praised him "for acting ...with promptitude and intelligence," and promised that New Caledonia would soon receive colonial status. In the meantime, Douglas was on his own. A repetition of the American takeover of Oregon looked very likely. As Douglas warned London, "If the majority of immigrants be American, there will always be a hankering in their minds after annexation to the United States. ... They will never cordially submit to English rule, nor possess the loyal feelings of British subjects."

The British population of Victoria was less than five hundred, and of the whole island only about one thousand. They would scarcely counterbalance the newcomers. In addition, Victoria was contending with a permanent labor shortage; it was a nuisance now, but would be paralyzing when the Californians flooded in. The lack of skilled manpower was so severe that when a small military detachment was sent out to survey the international boundary that spring, Douglas told London that the soldiers would be difficult to accommodate: "The floating population of this Colony have, with very few exceptions, wandered off to the newly discovered gold diggings at Thompson's River, and there will therefore be great difficulty, unless the mines prove a failure, in engaging local white labour. Indian labourers can however be engaged in any number required though it would not be advisable to employ a large proportion of that class of labourers, as they are a rather unruly force, requiring very close and constant supervision." What the colony needed, obviously, was a sizable group of hardworking settlers who were not Americans — settlers who would be loyal to the Crown. And it needed them in a matter of weeks.

Aware of events in San Francisco, Douglas must have known of the growing discontent of its Black community. Here was a relatively large, cohesive group of industrious people. Since the U.S. Supreme Court's Dred Scott decision in 1857, slavery had been upheld and even free Blacks had been denied the hope of citizenship in their native land. Such people would certainly not feel "a hankering in their minds after annexation to the United States if they were to settle in British territory; they could serve as a useful counterweight to the American influx Douglas expected.

It seems likely, therefore, that Douglas himself sent the invitation which Captain Nagle presented to the San Francisco Black community in mid-April of 1858. No one else in the colony would have had the authority to do so; no one else would have seen the urgent need for such settlers; and no one else would have dared to proffer such an invitation without both Douglas's knowledge and approval.

What is certain is that the invitation arrived at the precise moment when the Blacks were poised to act. It was decisive. Within a few days of Archy Lee's release, he and the rest of the Pioneer Committee stepped off the *Commodore* onto British soil.

CHAPTER THREE

"A God-sent land for the colored people"

Forty years afterward, Dr. John Sebastian Helmcken recalled an episode involving his father-in-law, James Douglas, and its aftermath: "He showed us a soda-water bottle half-full of scaly gold, which had been collected I think by the Indians in the North Thompson. The Legislature existed at this period, but took no heed of these discoveries. One Sunday morning we were astonished to find a steamer entering the harbor from San Francisco. There was a regular colony of colored men on board, who had come to settle in Vancouver Island, because at this time adverse feeling ran high against them in the States. They landed and some kneeling down prayed and asked blessing on those who lived in freedom under the red white and blue."

In this one paragraph, Helmcken struck the major themes of the Blacks' experience in British Columbia. The legislature had done nothing because Douglas himself did everything. The tiny colony was unprepared for the miners in general and the Blacks in particular. The Blacks were ready to bless their new country at first sight, to project their hopes onto a land and people that might not be able to sustain them. There is quiet, unintended irony in Helmcken's last sentence, and in the immigrants' prayers.

There had already been irony in the comments of the California press. On April 21, the day after the *Commodore* departed, the San Francisco *Daily Evening Bulletin* commented on the significance of the departure of the first Black emigrants: "All this puts one in mind of the Pilgrims...when those adventurers embarked for their new homes across the sea. When the colored people get their 'poet,' he will no doubt sing of these scenes which are passing around us almost unheeded, and the day when colored people fled persecution in California may yet be celebrated in story.... The sixty-five yesterday went off in the Commodore and are pushing up towards the north, bearing their *lares* and *penates* to found new homes.... Whatever may be their destiny, we hope the colored people may do well."

Kind though the writer's intentions may have been, his comparison of the Blacks to the Pilgrims and Romans probably inspired more guffaws than respect; it also served to mask the Blacks' plight in a veil of genteel literary allusion. When the paper came out, the advance party (Archy Lee among them) were sitting on a crowded deck among hundreds of white gold-seekers, trying to eat supper on a rough sea. They were additionally plagued by some young toughs who had stowed away and were now amusing themselves by kicking over the Blacks' mess kits.

It was a rough voyage in an unseaworthy old ship (later that summer, the *Commodore* escaped sinking off Point Reyes only by jettisoning all its cargo), but after five days they were safe in Victoria harbor. As their fellow-passengers invaded the town, seeking temporary shelter and the quickest possible transport to the mouth of the Fraser, the Pioneer Committee rented a room from a local carpenter for a prayer meeting.

One of the local residents who took an interest in the Blacks was the Reverend Edward Cridge, an Anglican minister. In his diary, he recorded their arrival and his first dealings with them: "On Sunday Apl 25 the Commodore Capt. Nagle, arrived with 400 or 500 Emigrants from San Francisco...There were also 35 men of colour from the same place of different trades and callings, chiefly intending to settle here. On Monday (Apl. 26) drinking tea at Mrs. Blinkhorn's with my wife she (Mrs. B.) told us that on the precedg evening she was surprised at hearing the sounds of praise. They proceeded from the men of colour who had taken a large room at Laing's the Carpenter; & they spent the Sabbath Evening in worshipping the word of God. On the following morning I called on them. They appeared much gratified by my visit.

I requested permission to ask them a few questions which they decidedly acceded to."

The Blacks told Cridge of the legal oppression they had endured in California, and of the threat of Bill 339. "They also told me that a deputation of three of their number had waited on the Governor who had given them a good reception and they were much encouraged by the statement he gave of the privileges they would here enjoy." These three were Fortune Richard, Wellington Moses (born in Britain), and a man named Mercier, who had been delegated to meet Douglas and report back to San Francisco.

When the Blacks told him "that they did not intend to establish a distinct Church organization at Victoria but to join to some Ch. already in existence here," Cridge invited them to attend his own church. Many of them did so over the next few weeks, and Cridge learned a good deal about their backgrounds. Several of them still had families in slavery, and hoped to earn enough in Victoria or the gold fields to buy their freedom.

The Pioneer Committee lost no time in getting settled. Many bought land in town; some formed a brickmaking company; others found work at once on the farms of white settlers, who were delighted to see them. Augustus Pemberton, an important settler who was later Commissioner of Police, hired several Blacks less than a week after their arrival; they split rails, cleared acres of land, and sheared sheep.

Mercier returned to San Francisco at the end of April and presented a detailed report on the colony to 350 listeners at Zion Church. The advance party, he said, had enjoyed a very good reception. Governor Douglas had made them welcome, and the delegates' meeting with him had been "very cheerful and agreeable." Douglas had given them a good deal of information about settling. Under the colony's laws, immigrants could buy land at one pound per acre — about five dollars. By American standards this was an outrageous price, as Douglas himself knew and regretted; it had been set by London bureaucrats ignorant of the costs of getting uncleared land into usable condition. Settlers could, however, make a 25 percent down payment, with the balance to be paid in four yearly instalments at 5 percent interest. Land would not be taxed until 1860.

After nine months, anyone owning land had the right to vote

and to sit on juries. While all immigrants would be protected by the laws, Douglas advised, settlers could not claim all the rights of British subjects until they had lived in the colony for seven years and then taken an oath of allegiance to the Crown. As the Blacks were to learn to their sorrow, this aspect of their status was not entirely accurate; but, coming as it did from the governor himself, no one questioned it. The prospect of enfranchisement was especially attractive to the Blacks, who had endured taxation without representation for generations.

Mercier also read a letter from Wellington Moses, who had already fallen in love with Vancouver Island: "To describe the beauty of the country my pen cannot do it. It is one of the most beautifully level towns I was ever in.... I consider Victoria to be one of the garden spots of this world.... The climate is most beautiful; the strawberry vines and peach trees are in full blow.... All the colored man wants here is ability and money.... It is a God-sent land for the colored people."

Such reports only added to the growing enthusiasm for emigration. A week later, at yet another meeting, it was proposed that an emigration society be formed, to recruit 100 members at $25 each. The society's governors would then charter a ship to transport the entire group to Victoria. It does not seem that such a society was actually formed, however; with a steamer ticket costing only $15 on the regular run, there was little need to charter a ship.

The meeting also passed twelve resolutions, preceded by a preamble both bitter and articulate: "Whereas, We are fully convinced that the continued aim of the spirit and policy of our mother country, is to oppress, degrade and outrage us. We have therefore determined to seek an asylum in the land of strangers from the oppression, prejudice and relentless persecution that have pursued us for more than two centuries in this our mother country. Therefore a delegation having been sent to Vancouver's Island, a place which has unfolded to us in our darkest hour, the prospect of a bright future; to this place of British possession, the delegation having ascertained and reported the condition, character, and its social and political privileges and its living resources. This mission in the highest creditable, they have fulfilled and rendered the most flattering accounts to their constituents in their report...."

Some of the following resolutions were simple courtesies: thanks to the delegation in Victoria, to Governor Douglas, and to Reverend Cridge. Others offered sound business advice to prospective settlers: invest in land. Still others were both an expression of social idealism and a politically thoughtful strategy. The Blacks committed themselves to integration with the white community, resolving not to form Black schools, churches, or social groups. As they would soon learn, however, acting as a bloc would gain them more influence than they ever dreamed, though at a high price.

The day after this meeting, all the African Methodist Episcopal ministers of San Francisco held a convention to discuss the impending migration. As one of them put it, "just when we were asking ourselves, 'Where shall we go?' God Himself came to our aid and opened the door for us." The ministers passed a resolution even more far-reaching than the last: "In the opinion of this convention we deem it expedient to call upon our people throughout California in particular, and the Atlantic States in general, to save all the money they can and prepare themselves to emigrate to a country where the color of their skin will not be considered a crime and where they can in fine, enjoy all the right and privileges which will alone make them a great and mighty people."

The renewed hope of the Blacks was expressed as well in a poem by a California Black woman who would soon join the emigrants:

"A Voice From the Oppressed to the Friends of Humanity"

Composed by one of the suffering class.
Mrs. Priscilla Stewart

Look and behold our sad despair
Our hopes and prospects fled,
The tyrant slavery entered here,
And laid us all for dead.

Sweet home! When shall we find a home?
If the tyrant says that we must go
The love of gain the reason,
And if humanity dare say "no".
Then they are tried for treason.

God bless the Queen's majesty,
Her sceptre and her throne,
She looked on us with sympathy,
And offered us a home.

Far better breathe Canadian air,
Where all are free and well,
Than live in slavery's atmosphere
And wear the chains of hell.

Farewell to our native land,
We must wave the parting hand,
Never to see thee any more,
But seek a foreign land.

Farewell to our true friends,
Who've suffered dungeon and death.
Who have a claim upon our gratitude
Whilst God shall lend us breath.

May God inspire your hearts,
A Marion raise your hands;
Never desert your principles
Until you've redeemed your land.

Less than two months after the freeing of Archy Lee, a whole community was on its way to Victoria.

CHAPTER FOUR

"If you go in blind you will come out skinned."

Throughout the spring and summer of 1858, the Black emigrants left San Francisco. They were only a fraction of the adventurers traveling north; the new gold rush seemed to be depopulating the Bay Area. Some San Franciscans even feared that their city would soon lose its economic supremacy to Victoria. "San Francisco," the *Daily Evening Bulletin* observed in June, "is running wild with excitement." Everyone wanted news from the north; the *Bulletin* printed a map of the Fraser River several times, as well as a glossary of Chinook Jargon, the trade language of the Northwest.

"The Pacific Mail Steamship office was this morning completely besieged with applicants for tickets to Frazer River. The American Exchange and Wharf House are running over. The house of J.M. Strobridge, the great head-quarters of the Clothing trade, presented the busiest scene of all." So ran one account. The *Bulletin* sounded almost plaintive when it editorialized: "It is to be hoped that our people will not permit themselves to become so completely absorbed in Frazer River speculations as to suffer the approaching Fair of the State Agricultural Society to pass thinly attended."

Nevertheless, the San Francisco papers did their best to distract their readers from everything but the gold rush. Mifflin Gibbs helped contribute to the excitement through a letter published in the *Bulletin* on June 23:

"Victoria, V.I., June 16, 1858

Friend L [probably Peter Lester]: — You will now see that I have arrived at my point of destination. I came, however, rather late to make the most advantageous investments. The country is certainly a beautiful one — a country good enough for me — and I am sorry we are so far behind. If either of us had arrived here two months ago, worth $1,000, we could have been worth $10,000 today. As it is, I arrived here (or on land) on Saturday, 12th June, and the Land Office closed on Friday, for ten days, completely shutting off all purchasers for that time. I went to the office, and was introduced to the officers. They informed me that they would give public notice when the office opened, and I would have a fair chance. The lots have been selling at $50, but when the office opens I understand they will be $100. They said they had to close in order to regulate matters, as the lots were being sold faster than they could be surveyed, and would get confused. On the last day, the office was literally besieged. They took some forty or fifty thousand dollars.

"I have been terribly bothered and almost bewildered, not knowing how to act. There are a number of lots in the hands of half-a-dozen speculators, who are holding them at exorbitant rates. Lots in the most desirable portion of the town at this time, which could have been bought from the Land Office, three months ago, for $50, and from settlers here for from $300 to $700, they are now asking, and getting, from $1,500 to $5,000 for. A lot sold since I have been here (three days) for $5,000, has again changed hands for $6,200. Everybody is excited; but I think that real estate is as high as it can safely be. It will undoubtedly go higher, but will first recede to await the immigration of actual settlers. The fact is, that there is the greatest possible demand for houses, both to live and do business in, in the business portion of the town. Men are walking around, begging for a place to live and do business in. All the lots are sold to within four squares of the business quarter, and further I guess.

"The business portion here is generally owned by old fogies, who are destitute of Yankee enterprise. They are afraid to lease, for fear they will regret it; and ask such prices that parties who have the means are afraid to buy. Add to this that you cannot purchase a piece of lumber in the place, that houses half-way in the process of erection are standing idle, and that there are no sloops or scows in the harbor to go after it. A great many miners, who are waiting here for the river to fall, have camped around the tents. Lumber here would now fetch $60 to $100 a thousand. I have not had my clothes off nor had a bed to lie on, since I left San Francisco. I thought I would have broke down the first day or two, not having had a night's comfortable rest since I left. Then landing in a whirlpool of excitement! But I am feeling better now, and am getting pretty thoroughly posted on land points and specu- lators, and that is worth considerable, for if you go in blind you will come out skinned.... I have said nothing about the mines, as people here have ceased to ask any questions on that point; their permanency and richness are undoubted by all who arrive from them."

Gibbs's letter conveys the feverish mood of Victoria in its first boom. A small, quiet hamlet, it had been staggered by huge num- bers of newcomers, most of them transients. One who came to stay, Alfred Waddington, described the shock in his book *The Fraser Mines Vindicated* (the first book published in Victoria); before the rush, he wrote, Victoria had been a backwater: "No noise, no bustle, no gamblers or speculators or interested parties to preach up this or underrate that. A few quiet gentlemanly behaved inhabitants, chiefly Scotchmen, secluded as it were from the whole world.... As to business there was none, the streets were grown over with grass, and there was not even a cart."

Waddington confirmed Gibbs's first impressions of the influx of miners: "This immigration was so sudden, that people had to spend their nights in the streets or bushes, according to choice, for there were no hotels sufficient to receive them. Victoria had at last been discovered, everybody was bound for Victoria, nobody could stop anywhere else, for there, and there alone, were fortunes, and large fortunes, to be made....

"Never perhaps was there so large an immigration in so short a space of time into so small a place. Unlike California, where the distance from the Eastern States and Europe precluded the possi-

bility of an immediate rush, the proximity of Victoria to San Francisco, on the contrary, afforded every facility, and converted the
whole matter into a fifteen dollar trip....

"As to goods, the most exorbitant prices were asked and realized;
for though the Company had a large assortment, their store in the
Fort was literally besieged from morning to night; and when all
were in such a hurry, it was not every one that cared to wait three
or four hours, and sometimes half a day, for his turn to get in.
The consequence was, that the five or six stores that were first
established did as they pleased."

As well as the miners, the rush attracted many anxious entrepreneurs like Gibbs: "An indescribable array of Polish Jews, Italian
fishermen, French cooks, jobbers, speculators of every kind, land
agents, auctioneers, hangers on at auctions, bummers, bankrupts,
and brokers of every description.... To the above lists may be added
a fair seasoning of gamblers, swindlers, thieves, drunkards, and
jail birds, let loose by the Governor of California for the benefit
of mankind, besides the halt, lame, blind, and mad. In short,
the outscourings of a population containing, like that of California,
the outscourings of the world."

Victoria stands on a small harbor in a beautiful setting. To the
south, across Juan de Fuca Strait, the sharp white peaks of the
Olympic Range rise dramatically into the sky. On clear days, one
can look eastward to the immense cone of Mount Baker, a dor-
mant volcano on the American mainland across Georgia Strait;
the Strait itself is dotted with green islands. Victoria today is one
of the loveliest and most comfortable cities in North America, but
in the summer of 1858 it must have been a singularly unpleasant
place, despite the scenery and the praise of Wellington Moses.
The old settlers' small, whitewashed cottages were now surrounded
by jerrybuilt shanties and hundreds of tents. The once-grassy
streets were quagmires so deep that everyone — even ladies — wore
high boots. And though the Northwest is notoriously rainy, water
was scarce and expensive — a nickel a bucket.

The town was also crowded with Indians, whose encampments
ringed the settlement. Haidas, Bella Bellas, Tsimshians, Kwakiutl,
Coast Salish and others visited Victoria to trade, gossip, work, or
simply enjoy the excitement. The arrival of thousands of white
men — many willing to pay inflated prices for sex as for everything

else — put irresistible pressure on many Indian women to become prostitutes. The venereal diseases they contracted soon spread widely, and contributed to a steep drop in the Indian birthrate.

Matthew Macfie, a Congregationalist minister, was appalled at the sordid effects of Indian prostitution: "...the crowds of the more debased miners strewed in vicious concert with squaws on the public highway presented a spectacle diabolical in the extreme. Even now one cannot walk from the ferry up the Esquimalt Road by day or night without encountering the sight of these Indian slaves squatting in considerable numbers in the bush, for what purpose it is not difficult to imagine, and the extent to which the nefarious practices referred to are encouraged by crews of Her Majesty's ships is a disgrace to the service they represent, and a scandal to the country. Hundreds of dissipated white men, moreover, live in open concubinage with these wretched creatures. So unblushingly is this traffic carried on, that I have seen the husband and wife of a native family canvassing from one miner's shanty to another, with the view of making assignations for the *clootchmen* (squaws) in their possession."

In all this uproar, Gibbs and the other Blacks worked frantically to settle themselves. Gibbs had not exaggerated the scope of land speculation. The government itself was legally forbidden to sell land in parcels smaller than 20 acres; town and suburban lots were sold by the HBC and private owners, who soon grew rich. As Waddington described it, "one half of a fifty dollar corner lot, the whole of which had been offered successively for 250, 500, 750, and 1000 dollars, and finally sold for 1100 dollars, was resold a fortnight afterwards, that is to say the half of it, for 5000 dollars. Old town lots, well situated, brought any price, and frontages of 20 and 50 feet, by 60 deep, rented from 250 to 400 dollars per month."

Bothered and bewildered though he may have been, Gibbs landed on his feet. He had come north with a sizable stock of miners' supplies; it was snapped up at prices far higher than San Francisco's, and he at once ordered more. He then put $100 down on a lot and house; the total price was $3,000, with $1,400 to be paid in two weeks and the rest in six months. As a boy in Philadelphia he had worked in carpentry, a trade that now stood him in good stead, for he was able to remodel the house himself. Once it was divided into two units, he rented one out for $500. The other unit became the premises of a firm whose ads were soon running in the Victoria *Gazette:*

Lester & Gibbs
Dealers in Groceries, Provisions,
Boots, Shoes, &c.,

Wholesale & Retail

L. & G. having permanently established
themselves in Victoria, would respectfully
call the attention of Families, Miners
and the public generally to their very
superior stock, to which they are receiving
additions by every arrival.
N.B. — Consignments solicited, and attended
to with promptness and despatch.

The firm was the Hudson's Bay Company's first competitor in Victoria, and therefore among that happy group of businesses that, as Waddington put it, "did as they pleased." Gibbs could soon buy a five-acre suburban lot at Michigan and Menzies in the James Bay district (named by the Governor for himself), build a house, and hire an Indian manservant.

Other Blacks were also setting up in business. Nathan Pointer, who had been Gibbs's first partner in San Francisco, opened a large clothing store. Wellington Moses was soon running the Pioneer Shaving Saloon and Bath Room (Private Entrance for Ladies); he and other Blacks virtually monopolized barbering. Fortune Richard worked as a ship carpenter. Archy Lee, who had helped start the exodus, found work first as a porter and later as a drayman. A Virginian named Joshua Howard advertised himself as an "Attorney and Counsellor at Law...Advice in law, to the poor gratis."

Some of Victoria's new restaurants and saloons were owned and run by Blacks. According to James K. Nesbitt, the best restaurant in town was Ringo's, on Yates Street. Nesbitt quotes a writer in the 1880s: "Every notable who came to Victoria in those days was escorted to Ringo's for a square meal. This was considered the highest mark of hospitality." Samuel Ringo, a big, gentle man, had been a slave most of his life. After nursing his master through an attack of smallpox, Ringo had contracted the disease himself; when he recovered, his grateful master freed him. Blacks and whites alike patronized his restaurant, but for all its prestige its customers were often rowdy. On one occasion, a man left his shiny new plug hat on the counter while he enjoyed his meal. "When he came to replace the hat on his head, his horror may be imagined to find the juice of half a dozen eggs, and the oil from a pound of soft butter, trickling down his face." A year or two later, according to the same writer, two American customers—sympathizers with opposing sides in the U.S. Civil War—got into an argument. "Blows were exchanged and pistols drawn. Ringo, in the kitchen, heard the row, and running out threw his great long arms about both men and gathered them to his greasy breast. He held them there as in a vise, until they consented to put up their pistols and shake hands."

Within a very short time, Blacks were engaged in work at every level of the colony's economy, from manual labor to the professions. For a few weeks in June 1858 they even policed Victoria. Douglas himself seems to have appointed them, perhaps as a way of reminding American whites that they were on British soil. Most were Jamaicans, and all were British subjects. Despite their impressive uniforms—blue coats, red sashes, and high hats—the new constables met immediate resistance. In one incident, a thief caught red-handed in a miner's tent admitted his guilt but refused to be taken to jail by a Black man. Enough of his fellow-whites backed him up to make an arrest impossible. After several such episodes, most of the Black policemen were withdrawn from service. One, Lorne Lewis, stayed on for several years as constable for the Songhees Indian Reserve outside Victoria.

The social backgrounds of the Blacks were varied. Some, like Archy Lee, were southern-born ex-slaves; others, like Gibbs, were freeborn northerners who regarded themselves as self-starting Yankees. Some were well educated: John Craven Jones and his brothers William and Elias were graduates of Oberlin College in Ohio, and Fielding Smithea had also attended Oberlin. Many, including Gibbs, were self-educated; others were illiterate or nearly so. While most had been born in the United States, a sizable minority of the Blacks were British subjects born in the West Indies or Britain itself.

Diverse though they were in their origins and abilities, the Black pioneers were, in general, tough, resourceful, aggressive and ambitious. It is rarely remembered that migration from the eastern U.S. to California was difficult for any but people with money and boldness; for Blacks, the journey had been even harder. And to succeed in a white-ruled frontier state had demanded brains, talent, and courage. By a rigorous self-selection process, therefore, only the best-adapted Blacks reached Victoria and the gold fields.

The white society in which the Black immigrants found themselves was undergoing rapid change. F.E. Walden, a historian of British Columbia's early days, has outlined its basic structure:

"The British governing clique held firmly to its position as the upper class in Victoria. Governor Douglas and the succeeding governors, their wives and families, entertained the high supporting officials of the colony, most of whom were resident in Victoria. High-ranking officers of the Royal Navy and the Royal Engineers were included in this circle, and junior officers of the Services provided suitable escorts for the young ladies of these families. High officials of the Hudson's Bay Company completed this ruling hierarchy. Only slightly below ranked the professional section of the population, consisting almost entirely of British doctors, lawyers and clergy.

"The bulk of the population formed what might be properly called a 'healthy middle class,' or proprietary group, led by American and Jewish merchants. With various German, Negro and British shop-keepers, this group took an active and growing part in municipal affairs, political, economic and social. Supporting this middle class were the skilled tradesmen of nearly every nationality, although as a group they did not make their influence felt to any great extent.

"Caste division as it applied to the labouring population transcended the bounds of nationalities, and the opportunity to advance into the ranks of the merchant section grew. German, Italian, Negro, Indian, Chinese and Kanaka household servants formed

Mifflin Wistar Gibbs

Sir James Douglas

Amor De Cosmos

Sir Matthew Baillie Begbie

A sugar sculpture caricaturing B.C. delegates to the Yale Convention

Mrs. Peter Lester

Peter Lester

Samuel Booth

Samuel Booth, Mason and gold seeker

Baker Robert Clanton

Victoria Richard Clanton

Mary Lowe Barnswell

James Barnswell, carpenter

The "African Rifles," formally known as the Victoria Pioneer
Rifle Company

Fielding William Spotts, of
Saltspring Island and Saanich

Fielding Spotts, Jr., a well known
Vancouver figure of the 1920s and '30s

Charles and Nancy Alexander

Willis Stark and Jim Anderson, another Saltspring Island farmer

A Saltspring Island hotel mural depicts John Craven Jones teaching the pioneers' children

Philip Sullivan

Richard Stokes, who kept a livery stable on Broughton Street in Victoria in the 1870s

Mrs. John T. Pierre

Josephine Sullivan

Seraphim ("Joe") Fortes

the large proportion of this group of semi-skilled and unskilled labour at the bottom of the social scale."

A contemporary observer, Rev. Matthew Macfie, saw Victoria's society somewhat differently: "The Government officials," he wrote in 1865, "constitute the centre of the social system (still in a formative state), and around it multitudes of broken-down gentlemen and certain needy tradespeople rotate. The most wealthy members of the community have, in general, more money than culture — a condition of things always incident to the early stage of colonial development. Many of them owe their improved circumstances simply to being the lucky possessors of real estate at a time when it could be bought for a nominal amount. Some who eight years ago were journeymen smiths, carpenters, butchers, bakers, public-house keepers or proprietors of small curiosity shops in San Francisco or Victoria, are now in the receipt of thousands of pounds a year."

The British-born Macfie was struck by the lack of a firm class structure in the new colony: "The immigrant accustomed to the distinctions of class obtaining in settled populations of the old world, will be struck to observe how completely the social pyramid is inverted in the colonies. Many persons of birth and education, but of reduced means, are compelled, for a time after their arrival, to struggle with hardship, while the vulgar, who have but recently acquired wealth, are arrayed in soft clothing and fare sumptuously. Sons of admirals and daughters of clergymen are sometimes found in abject circumstances, while men only versed in the art of wielding the butcher's knife, the drayman's whip, and the blacksmith's hammer, or women of low degree, have made fortunes." He cited the case of a gentleman charged with being drunk and disorderly; the arresting constable was his own former manservant. Macfie also took amused note of the number of apparent fugitives from justice: "Druggists inform me that the demand for hair-dye by immigrants is so large as to be quite noticeable. The cause of this expedient, in such a country, may be readily conjectured."

Amid all this social upheaval, most of the British-born elite found the Blacks an island of stability. Rev. William F. Clarke, a Canadian-born Congregational missionary, said of them that "a large proportion...are very respectable and intelligent; indeed as a whole they are superior to any body of coloured people with whom it has been my lot to meet." Lady Franklin, widow of the Arctic explorer Sir John Franklin, met many of the Blacks when she visited Victoria in 1861, and her niece, Sophia Cracroft, described them as "a most orderly and useful and loyal section of the community...they certainly do speak with a propriety & degree of refinement which is peculiar to their race, & certainly superior to the same rank among Englishmen."

A somewhat more patronizing tone, however, is evident in a description of the Blacks by Lt. R.C. Mayne of the Royal Navy, who was stationed at Esquimalt Harbour near Victoria during the gold rush: "As a rule these free negroes are a very quiet people, a little given perhaps to over familiarity when any opening for it is afforded, very fond of dignity, always styling each other Mr., and addicted to an imposing costume, in the way of black coats, gold studs and watch-chains, &c.; but they are a far more steady, sober and thrifty set than the whites by whom they are so much despised."

What comes through in these writers is an odd sort of tolerance born of social snobbery. As upper- and middle-class Britishers, they discriminated by class, not color; a solid merchant like Mifflin Gibbs therefore merited more respect than a laborer of any race. The somewhat absentminded goodwill of the British was probably due less to moral principle than to the fact that there were precious few Blacks in Britain.

Another reason for the British colonists' fairness toward the Blacks was that, overwhelmed in number by the white Americans, who now formed the great majority of Victoria's inhabitants, the British elite soon found that such expressions of tolerance helped set them apart from men they saw as uncouth, hypocritical, vulgar upstarts. Douglas himself seems to have taken a certain reserved pleasure in needling the Americans, and not only on the race issue; just before the gold rush, for example, he had blandly declined to return two U.S. Army deserters to Washington Territory.

Some of the Black immigrants, of course, were as tough and brutal as some of their white neighbors. One Black teamster, trying to get a wagon through the muddy streets, lost his temper and beat his horse to death. Other Blacks were notorious brawlers and thieves, and one or two were suspected of murder. Some sold whisky to the Indians and were regular patrons of the whorehouses on Cormorant Street. Yet in proportion to their total numbers, the Blacks who broke the law were a very small group indeed. On balance, James Douglas could scarcely have made a better choice of settlers.

Despite the government's support for them, the Blacks soon felt the need to put their case to the public. In February 1859, Rev. J.J. Moore—one of the San Francisco clergymen who had supported the emigration—published a letter in the *Colonist* to explain the motives of the Black settlers. After cautioning his readers not to expect the Blacks to act as a unit, Moore outlined the predicament they had faced in California and went on to say: "…from this prejudice we have fled to a country governed by a nation far-famed for justice and humanity. Hasty fortunes we seek not; with some of us losses have been sustained, that the chief advantages of the country cannot briefly indemnify; but this is a secondary consideration with us: the full, free, and peaceable enjoyment of those highest inherent rights with which Heaven has gifted man, is the crowning thought with us, not dollars and cents…. We come here not to seek social favors, but to enjoy those common social rights that civilized, enlightened, and well regulated communities guarantee to all their members. We come not to seek any particular associations—(those of us who understand ourselves;) we only desire social rights in common with other men…. We have come to this country to make it the land of our adoption for ourselves and our children. We have come to possess the soil; to till the earth; to reap its productions, extract its minerals; to mould its rocks and forests into firesides; and to fill the solitary places with joy and gladness; …and build up for ourselves and children happy homes in the land of the free and the home of the brave."

Other groups were establishing themselves at the same time. One sea captain remarked that Victoria's population was racially more varied than that of any other port he had ever seen. Hawaiians arrived in considerable numbers; so did the first of the Chinese. East Indians, Chileans, Mexicans, and Europeans of all nationalities mingled in Victoria's streets and encampments. But white Americans predominated, and showed their attitude to other races in sometimes brutal ways: one Chinese immigrant, passing by some white miners on his way to get water, was shot five times without provocation.

In Victoria's fluid society, the Blacks soon struck roots and began to flourish. Many of their fellow-immigrants were transients, or too unstable to contribute much to the colony; the Blacks became "the 'old families' and monied aristocracy," as Macfie called them. Yet it was precisely their social virtues that led them into repeated conflicts with the white society around them. The first of these conflicts was religious, and Reverend Macfie was in the thick of it.

CHAPTER FIVE

"Shall white men or niggers rule in this colony?"

L ate in 1858, the mainland was proclaimed the Crown Colony of British Columbia; James Douglas was its first governor, but spent most of his time in Victoria, which still had the largest concentration of settlers in either of the colonies. The town had gone through a mild depression at the end of the summer; the melting snowpack had raised the Fraser, covering the gold-rich sand bars, and thousands of impatient miners had returned in frustration to Victoria, proclaiming the mines a "humbug." While they waited for passage home to San Francisco, some of them staged riots that were put down only after sailors were marched in from Esquimalt.

By autumn, however, the miners who had persisted on the Fraser were sending considerable amounts of gold across Georgia Strait, and prospectors began exploring the Fraser's tributaries with good results. So, though Victoria never again experienced the explosive growth of the '58 rush, it prospered. The Blacks prospered with it.

As most of them were deeply religious, church was an important part of their lives. The Rev. Edward Cridge had invited the Pioneer Committee to attend his services, and many did so. Not all the white parishioners welcomed them, however. One — an American named Sharpstone — published a protest in the *Gazette* in August, 1858:

"Last Sabbath was an unusually warm day. The little chapel was crowded as usual with a 'smart sprinkle' of blacks, *generously* mixed in with the whites. The Ethiopians *perspired!* they always do when out of place. Several white gentlemen left their seats vacant, and sought the purer atmosphere outside; others moodily endured the *aromatic luxury* of their positions, in no very pious frame of mind." Sharpstone urged that a section be set aside for the Blacks, "as is done in respectable churches in the world."

Next day, Mifflin Gibbs responded to the American's complaint. He handled Sharpstone, as one pioneer recalled, "without gloves." After stating that the church as well the government was only living up to its principles, Gibbs observed: "This seems to have awakened the negro-hating spirit of Alias Sharpstone and others of his ilk — as has been manifested by their uneasiness on the last few Sabbaths — proving that such persons are as destitute of Christian feeling as they are of the common principles of gentility. They visit church on each returning Sabbath — they live under and are protected in their persons and property by the government, and they neither pay a cent for the support of the one or the other. Yet, uninvited, mere pensioners on the bounty and liberality of this government, they have the unblushing effrontery to dictate to the powers that be what line of policy they shall pursue, and recommend a course which it is as impudent to suggest as it would be unjust and inimical to British principles to adopt.

"As for the silly twaddle about 'Ethiopian perspiration,' 'aromatic luxury,'...&c., it has long become obsolete even in the United States, and only writers of small calibre and low conceptions resort to it, as it proves nothing, save a dangerous weapon to handle — since the same perspiration and aromatic luxury (if it peculiarly exists in the negro) is not only endured, but apparently enjoyed by some of these carpers when Venus is the star of their adoration. It comes with a bad grace from Americans to talk of the horrors of amalgamation when every plantation of the South is more or less a seraglio, and numbers of the most prominent men in the State of California have manifested little heed to color in their choice of companions in an amorous intrigue or a nocturnal debauch."

The editor of the *Gazette* tried to end the dispute at this point, claiming that "Our space is not so extended as to permit giving much of it to questions of slight importance and minor interest." But there was more to come.

Cridge himself also wrote to the *Gazette*, and reproved his congregation for its intolerance. Some whites thereupon left the church, while others resorted to awkward strategems to put distance between themselves and the Blacks. Matthew Macfie, though not involved in this phase of the religious dispute, seems to have caught the tone of the whites' arguments:

"Many...remonstrated with the clergyman [Cridge] against allowing the congregation to assume a speckled appearance—a spectacle deemed by them novel and inconvenient. They insisted that they were prepared to treat the 'blacks' with the utmost humanity and respect, in their own place; but that the Creator had made a distinction which it was sinful to ignore; that the promiscuous arrangement might lead to the sexes in both races falling in love with each other, entering into marriage, and thus occasioning the deterioration of the whites without the elevation of the negroes being effected."

Cridge responded with firmness and integrity, which Macfie chose to portray as naiveté: "The worthy parson, being direct from the parent country, and till then wholly inexperienced in the social relations of the conflicting races...maintained that the stains of men's sin, in common, were so dark, that mere difference in colour was an affair of supreme insignificance before the Almighty, in comparison, and that the separation desired by the whites was of carnal suggestion, which Christianity demanded should be repressed. He is said even to have gone so deeply into the subject in a particular sermon as to assert that the disposition of nerves, tendons, and arteries, and the essential faculties of the soul were alike in white and black—the sole distinction between them consisting of colouring matter under the skin, the projection of the lower jaw, and the wool by which the scalp was covered."

The issue simmered for several months, and then erupted in another church—the mission established by Rev. William F. Clarke, a Canadian-born Congregationalist. Early in 1859, the Congregational Unions of England and Canada had appointed him to undertake the mission to Vancouver Island; arriving that summer, he found Victoria somewhat disappointing. He had been told there were eight to ten thousand inhabitants; the actual number was closer to three thousand.

In addition to Cridge's Anglican church, there were several other flourishing denominations, as well as many groups impervious to Congregationalism: "Roman Catholics, English, Irish, German, and French; Jews, Chinamen, and others each claim a share of the population," he wrote, "leaving but a small residuum accessible to us.... I have not yet discovered in Victoria a single English Congregationalist, although I have searched the place almost microscopically for such a *rara avis*. I find three American Congregationalists...but the permanence of their stay here is not yet settled."

Nonetheless, Clarke worked hard to establish his mission. In a town where housing was as scarce for worshipers as for miners, he managed to rent a "barn-like upper-room" for $25 a month, and raised enough money from collections to furnish it. Within a month after his arrival, he was preaching to as many as 140 people and running a Sunday school with 31 students.

In his last appointment, in Wisconsin, Clarke had been an outspoken enemy of slavery, and his reputation had preceded him to Victoria. Perhaps for this reason, he soon attracted a sizable number of Blacks to his services. But his very first congregation also included some whites who, the following day, asked him what he intended to do about the fact that Blacks had sat intermingled with the others.

"Nothing," Clarke retorted.

Indignant, the whites told him they would have nothing more to do with his mission, and warned him that his whole congregation would soon be Black.

"Be it so, then," Clarke said. "Better it should be so, than introduce an odious, foolish, sinful feeling such as this, to 'the throne of supremacy,' in the house and over the worship of God."

Clarke adamantly told his congregation he would have nothing to do with a "negro corner." The Blacks were as much sons of God as the whites, he said, and he praised their determination "to seek those equal religious privileges to which they are by natural right and gospel grant, entitled."

The results of his stand were as he had been warned; in less than a month, Clarke's congregations were half Black — "possibly sometimes a larger proportion." He persisted, advising his superiors that it would be better for the mission to fail than to survive by segregation.

At this point Rev. Matthew Macfie, of the Congregational Union in Britain, arrived in Victoria. He had been expected to cooperate with Clarke's mission; instead, he broke almost at once with the Canadian over the segregation issue and began holding separate services. The Canadian Congregationalists, upon learning of Macfie's move, were scandalized; the editor of the church's *Canadian Independent Magazine* attacked Macfie as being "in opposition to the work of a brother Agent already occupying the ground," and branded Macfie's attitude "anti-christian." Many of Clarke's Canadian supporters agreed, and sent him messages of encouragement. They also raised money to help him build his own church on a site donated by the Hudson's Bay Company.

Meanwhile, Clarke faced growing difficulties. His children were harassed for having a "nigger preacher" for a father and for having to sit with Blacks in church. Newcomers to town were systematically warned to avoid Clarke's services — "with the avowed intention," he wrote, "in 'Yankee-phrase,' to 'boost Macfie along,' and to 'drive Clarke out of Victoria.'"

Macfie's supporters also tried to "boost him along" by a petition to the Congregationalists' Colonial Missionary Society. Clarke wrote that signatures were obtained by taking the petition to a hotel frequented by American miners. "A ...speech was made to the crowd of them, the question put, 'shall white men or niggers rule in this Colony?' and on the white men being elected by acclamation to rule the country, all who were of that mind were invited to sign the document!"

It was clear that Clarke and his mission had been singled out as a political target, probably because of his anti-slavery reputation, for the Episcopalians and Methodists — who also integrated Black and white worshipers — had no trouble over the issue. Had he been in a stronger position, with a large, loyal, and racially mixed congregation, Clarke could have succeeded; in fact, he would probably not have had to deal with the harassment at all. While his moral position was unquestioned, his finances were inadequate to a long siege; he was compelled, therefore, to abandon the mission in the spring of 1860. There were just not enough supporters. The Blacks admired him, but most were already in Reverend Cridge's fold. In any case, they did not intend to segregate themselves by driving whites away, and Clarke's mission had been stigmatized as "the black man's church."

Back in Toronto, Clarke fought a bitter battle with the committee of the Colonial missionary society, which waffled on the dispute between the two clergymen and on the segregation issue in general. The committee blamed Clarke for causing the dispute; he in turn pointed out that until Macfie's arrival no church had segregated its worshipers. Clarke continued to criticize the committee in the pages of the church magazine for some months. Not until October 1860 did Macfie present his side of the story.

"When I preached for Mr. Clarke," Macfie wrote in the *Canadian Independent Magazine,* "the first Sunday after entering the Colony, I was amazed to find so large a proportion of the congregation made up of coloured people.... When the two races are numerous, they are set apart in places of worship. But Mr. Clarke flattered himself he could revolutionize public sentiment on this point, though deeply rooted for ages, and he made it *primary*. I argued the subject with him kindly, and suggested a change of policy to give the whites, who form the staple of the Colony, a chance of hearing the gospel.... I took no part in discussing whether the prejudice was well founded or not; I simply treated it as a matter with which we, as public teachers, had nothing to do. I held that we could not afford to offend people by introducing innovations. I thought that if the whites would not sit side by side with blacks, they should rather be humoured with their own familiar arrangements than driven from the church altogether."

This letter had already been seen by the Colonial Missionary Society, together with Macfie's other correspondence, in which he had expanded on his own policy: "If negroes were pleased to give their attendance, they would be expected to take one side of the building, where they would be welcome to any unoccupied place they might choose, and where they would always find a number of whites sufficiently indifferent to the prejudice to sit in proximity to them."

Macfie had made his position entirely too clear for the Society, which ordered him to ensure "freedom of access...to every part of the building to all persons, without distinction of colour." If Macfie refused, "the connection of the Colonial Missionary Society must cease...."

But the order was a dead letter in any case. Clarke was gone. The Blacks refused to attend Macfie's church "to be put in the nigger's corner." Presumably Macfie found it easy to accept the Society's order, for he stayed on in Victoria for several years until at last his mission was closed down for financial reasons.

Macfie returned to Britain in the mid-1860s, both to raise funds for the church and to encourage emigration to British Columbia. In 1865 he published *Vancouver Island and British Columbia,* including in it an account of the religious dispute from which he himself was conspicuously absent:

"...a zealous Nonconformist fresh from the anti-slavery 'platform' in Canada, hastened to espouse the cause of the African. The coloured people, proud of so able a champion, rallied round him, and soon outnumbered the white adherents in his congregation.... This preponderance of colour in the chapel, however, did not accord with the objects the negroes were ambitious of attaining. They gradually withdrew to the fashionable church where they could enjoy the satisfaction of mingling more largely with the superior race; and, like the ass in the fable, between the two bundles of hay, the devoted friend of the African was thus starved out. So ungratefully are the disinterested services of philanthrophy sometimes requited! Many were of the opinion that a difficulty of so exceptional an order might have been successfully overcome by more prudent reticence on the part of these conscientious ministers. ...A little good nature, cautious management, and expedient neutrality on the part of the clergy, would, I have no doubt, soon have brought the antagonists to a proper understanding, and silenced the strife for precedence in the religious assembly."

Tedious though Macfie's archaic hypocrisy may be to readers already burdened with its modern equivalent, it is worth considering if only because many other whites shared it. He devotes an inordinate space in his book to discussing the races in the colony, with special concern expressed about the threat of miscegenation: "...I have known Europeans married to pure squaws, Indian half-breeds, and Mulatto females respectively. One case has come under my consideration of a negro married to a white woman, and another of a man descended from a Hindoo mother married to a wife of Indian extraction. A gentleman of large property, reported to be of Mulatto origin, is married to a half-breed Indian. From these heterogeneous unions, and from illicit commerce between the races just enumerated, it is evident that our population

cannot escape the infusion of a considerable hybrid offspring."
This passage is all the more churlish when we consider that the
"gentleman of large property" is almost certainly James Douglas
himself; Macfie seems to have had a gift for cowardly malice.

Like other racists of his time and our own, Macfie oscillated
between professions of admiration for nonwhites and grim warnings against them: "Does the presence, so largely, of inferior races
forbode the fatal tainting of the young nation's blood and signal
its premature decay, or will the vitality of the governing race triumph over the contamination with which more primitive types
threaten to engulf it?"

While Macfie had pandered to racism, other churchmen regarded him with distaste. The Right Reverend George Hills, first
Bishop of Columbia, criticized Macfie's "unchristian narrowness"
and praised Clarke for having "nobly upheld the Christian and
English sentiment; but his patrons have decided against him, and
he has to leave the place: he seems a very respectable man, too
good for his employers." The bishop also had high praise for the
Blacks. Though they made up only a fifth or sixth of Victoria's
population of three thousand, they accounted for no less than one
half of all churchgoing colonists, and showed themselves eager to
work for the church.

Yet even in the churches where they sat freely mingled with
whites, the Blacks encountered subtle discrimination. As a writer
in the *Colonist* observed in 1861, "Every Sabbath the Rev. Mr.
So-and-so gives out from his pulpit that the 'ladies' sewing circle
will meet at the residence of Mrs. — —. The male and female
members of the circle attend at the lady's house; but you never
see a black face, nor even that of a mulatto, among their number."

By the early 1860s, then, the Blacks had learned that justice
and equal treatment would have to be fought for here with as
much determination as in the United States. Despite their contribution to the colony's development — and the help of Victoria's
elite — they were still discriminated against. It was only natural
that they should take political action to protect their interests;
it was their misfortune, and the colony's, that their friends were
scoundrels and their enemies rascals.

CHAPTER SIX

"They always want a little more liberty than white men."

At the end of the 1850s, James Douglas was the governor of two separate colonies in the Northwest. Since the mainland colony of British Columbia was still thinly populated with a largely transient scattering of miners, he ruled there without interference from elected representatives. On Vancouver Island, however, rudimentary political institutions were growing rapidly. In the quiet days of 1856, the Vancouver Island House of Assembly had consisted of just seven men, elected by a handful of voters. The representative for Nanaimo, in fact, had been elected by a single voter, the only man in that little coal-mining hamlet with the required property qualification.

This first Assembly had been dissolved in the fall of 1859; its successor would reflect the changes the colony had undergone. Now there were nine electoral districts instead of four, and a total of fifteen representatives would be chosen. The electorate, though far larger, was still only a tiny fraction of the total population — the voters in Victoria Town, the largest district, could be listed in large type on less than one page of the *Colonist*.

Everyone realized that the election, scheduled for January 1860, would be a crucial one. The Hudson's Bay Company was no longer the power it had been, but its employees and supporters were still in control of the government. A growing class of newcomers, impatient to take over, grumbled over Douglas's policies and his manner of carrying them out. Many of these new voters were Englishmen or Canadians accustomed to "responsible government," which ruled only with the confidence of elected representatives. These newcomers also regarded the HBC as a dinosaurian relic of an earlier age, a protected monopoly in the century of laissez-faire capitalism. In their view, Douglas and his HBC henchmen would never give the colony the progressive, democratic government it deserved.

These newcomers found a spokesman late in 1858 in the editor-publisher of a new weekly paper, *The British Colonist*. He spelled out his principles in his first issue:

"In our National politics we shall ever foster that loyalty which is due to the parent government...Particular interest will be taken in the absorbing issues now before the British North American colonies: the union of these colonies, representation in the imperial parliament, the Pacific railroad...In our local politics we shall be found the sure friend of reform...We shall counsel the introduction of responsible government — a system long established in British America, by which the people will have the whole and sole control over the local affairs of the colony."

The editor was a Nova Scotian named Amor De Cosmos. Born William Alexander Smith, he had moved to California during the gold rush. He was a photographer and, by specializing in pictures of mining claims, he had prospered for several years in the camps and boom towns of California. For reasons still unclear, he applied to the state legislature for a change of name. He himself explained: "I desire not to adopt the name of Amor De Cosmos because it smacks of a foreign title, but because it is an unusual name and its meaning tells what I love most, viz.: order, beauty, the world, the universe."

The framers of the Civil Practice Act, delighted by the diversion Smith had afforded them, toyed with alternative names, and he was very nearly saddled with "Amor Muggins Cosmos" instead. It was later suggested that he had changed his name to evade the attention of the Vigilance Committees (hardly a sensible way to do so, if true), or simply to ensure prompter delivery of his mail in towns full of men named Bill Smith. Whatever the reason, he was Amor De Cosmos when he arrived in Victoria in the summer of 1858.

A tall, pale man with a long and glossy black beard, De Cosmos seems to have had no private life during his long residence in British Columbia. Except for land speculation and drinking (both of which he excelled at), he put all of his considerable energy and intelligence into public affairs; in the colony's early days, this was expressed as a violent and often libelous attack on Douglas's government.

Douglas, for all his abilities, was certainly an obvious target. He was a benevolent despot, but a despot nonetheless. The only limits on his power were the slack reins of the Colonial Office, the colony's perpetual lack of money, and the good sense of the naval officers whose warships were the only force he possessed to back up his authority. The governor was temperamentally remote from the idea of responsible government; he had not, after all, lived in a parliamentary state for forty years. His most recent exposure to a democracy had been the self-styled provisional government of the American settlers in Oregon. In Douglas's opinion, "people do not naturally take much interest in affairs of Government as long as affairs go on well and prosperously, and are content to leave questions of state to their ruling classes." In his time, the "ruling classes" had been the top men of the HBC. What was worse, his rising young men tended to marry into the Douglas family. Donald Cameron, Douglas's brother-in-law, was appointed the colony's first judge despite his utter lack of legal training; Dr. John Helmcken, who served for years as Speaker of the House of Assembly, was the HBC physician in the colony, and married one of Douglas's daughters.

When De Cosmos attacked the government as a "Family-Company Compact," therefore, he was on firm ground, and won a good deal of support for reform. Stung by this upstart's incessant criticism, Douglas tried clumsily to suppress the *British Colonist* by forcing De Cosmos to post a $2,500 bond. No doubt delighted at this gift of an issue, De Cosmos raised the money from his subscribers in just two days, and was soon hammering away at the governor with more energy than ever.

As 1859 drew to a close, De Cosmos could look back on a highly successful year. He was prosperous, famous, and influential; now he meant to carry his attack into the House of Assembly itself.

Douglas had had bitter enemies in the first Assembly, but they had been an ineffectual minority; the new representatives could pose a real threat to him. Whereas party politics were still far in the future, candidates in the 1860 election were generally identified as "Company" or "Reform." De Cosmos ran for one of Victoria Town's two seats; his opponents, both company supporters, were the 28-year-old Attorney General, George Hunter Cary, and auctioneer Selim Franklin.

Vancouver Island's voting laws were clumsy and already made obsolete by the colony's rapid growth. British subjects were the only ones allowed to vote; since there was no naturalization law, one could become a British subject only through birth or naturalization in Britain or some other colony, such as Nova Scotia or Jamaica. Such a subject must also hold enough property to qualify for the franchise. After he had registered as a voter, he might be challenged at a Court of Revision. This system was far from foolproof: unqualified voters sometimes stayed on the list only because no one challenged them, and some who did deserve to vote were prevented from doing so because they lacked proof of British citizenship.

Certainly this was not what Douglas had promised the Blacks' Pioneer Committee when he had told them that any property owner with nine months' residence could vote. No doubt many Black property owners soon learned of their actual unfranchised status, but in the fall of 1859 Attorney General Cary approached Gibbs with a very attractive idea. Since the U.S. Supreme Court's Dred Scott decision, Cary pointed out, had declared Blacks to be noncitizens, there was in consequence no naturalization problem for American-born Blacks in the colony. Any Black man meeting the property requirements could vote simply by swearing allegiance to the Queen.

The franchise had for generations been one of Black Americans' most desired privileges; when the Attorney General himself assured Gibbs that Blacks could vote, he saw no reason to ask questions. Over twenty Blacks therefore went to the sheriff's office, swore an oath of allegiance, and were duly registered. Although the registration period had ended, neither the sheriff nor the revisor raised any objections; they were company supporters.

De Cosmos raised no immediate protest either, though he could have. He may have hoped to gain the Black vote himself, for his editorials had supported them (especially in the church-segregation dispute) and had criticized white American bigotry. But if he did have such hopes, they were dead some weeks before the election, when he warned "the foreign portion" not to vote at all until passage of a naturalization bill would permit them to become British subjects.

On 7 January 1860, eighteen Blacks voted. There was no secret ballot; each voter stated his preference in public before the sheriff, who recorded the vote. It was soon clear that the Blacks were voting as a bloc for Cary and Franklin, and their votes were decisive. The final tally gave Cary 137, Franklin 106, and De Cosmos 91. Without his Black supporters, Franklin would have lost.

De Cosmos was furious, and a few days later published a long, bitter editorial on the perfidy of the Blacks and their white allies: "The colored people who have. . .controlled the election are not the only parties to blame. Coming hither from a country where no political rights are conceded to them, it is quite natural that they should eagerly accept every privilege offered them. The chief blame. . .belongs to the Attorney General." DeCosmos also implicated the sheriff, revisor, Chief Justice, and Douglas himself in the plot.

"We are heartily willing," De Cosmos continued, "That colored British-born citizens should fully enjoy all the rights of Englishmen.... We are also opposed to excluding colored foreigners from our soil. But it is in the nature of things unjust...that they should be allowed to vault upon the proud eminence of British citizenship, after a residence of four months in the colony. [This was almost surely a distortion; while a few of the black voters may have been such recent arrivals, most had been in Victoria for a year and a half.] There is rank absurdity as well as gross injustice in the idea of a colored man coming here fresh from slavery and gaining the franchise in four months.... We are quite aware of the ingenious plea set up in reference to the Dred Scott decision, which denies American citizenship to the colored man. But this decision does not make him less a foreigner.... Though disfranchised, they are still Americans."

Ominously, De Cosmos warned that the Blacks' triumph would

backfire: "The beşt friends of the colored people cannot but see
that what has taken place is calculated to do them injury, by pro-
voking a war of races, strengthening prejudice wherever it exists,
and rousing it where it has had no existence hitherto."

Had he confined his opinions to this editorial, De Cosmos would
have been unassailable. But he was Vancouver Island's leading
exponent of defamatory journalism, and he launched a vicious
anti-Black propaganda campaign with the same issue of the *Colonist*. A paragraph titled "The Ruling Powers" appeared just below
the editorial: "Carroll's bookkeeper was severely beaten on Saturday evening by some fifteen or twenty colored men at the Mous-
quetaire Saloon, corner of Government and Johnson Street." De
Cosmos also devoted a good deal of space in that issue to an eyewitness report on the "Colored-Cary-Franklin Jollification" held
the night after the election. The speech of Selim Franklin was
reported at length, but not necessarily with accuracy:

"Gentlemen, when I came to this country, it was not my intention to enter into politics, but after a short sojourn here, my friends,
the colored people, discovered my latent powers, as it were, and
found that I contained all the inherent qualities necessary to be a
good legislator, also that I was eminently fitted to nurture the
interests of the young Colony.' (Sensation.)...Mr. Franklin wished
to finish here, but a loud No! Go on! induced the speaker, after
applying a white handkerchief to his olfactory nerve, to resume
his eloquent discourse thus: — 'Gents, as I stated...my colored
friends placed me in the battle's van, and through them alone, I
am enabled to repeat the words of another great man, *veni, vidi,
vici.*' Here the speaker became exhausted (mentally)...Did Cary
and Franklin have any 'essence of Old Virginny' rubbed on their
coat tails as a decoy?

"Mr. Francis (colored) then arose amid a perfect shower of dust
and effluvia and recounted the Julius Caesaren [sic] deeds achieved
by the Anglo-African race &c. The speaker said, 'My father fought
at Trafalgar, and received medals. I have them in my possession
now. Gentlemen, I was determined to bring the colored influence
to bear against American prejudice. We have done it, and we
have achieved a victory. (Sensation.) Gentlemen, I have been
oppressed in the United States. I came to Victoria, and I found
an asylum. We came here knowing the Governor was favorable to

us, and that he was down on Englishmen who have been in California. Queen Victoria knows our worth, also that we are down on Yankees and that we'll fight them to the death. Put rifles in our hands, and we will fight the San Juan battles.'" (This last remark was an allusion to the dispute between Britain and the U.S. over ownership of San Juan Island, between Vancouver Island and Washington Territory.)

Unimpressed by these protestations of loyalty to the Crown, De Cosmos kept up his anti-Black campaign. A week after the election, the *Colonist* published a long letter over the pseudonym "Shears" — probably De Cosmos himself, to judge from the writer's style. Shears had little understanding of the Blacks' position, and saw their pro-Douglas vote as pure self-interest: "The only question they asked was, 'Who is most friendly to the "nigger," or who will promise most to the colored man?'" He went on to offer some generalizations with an altogether contemporary ring to them:

"The truth is — and the sooner it is told the better — the colored people do not know what are their rights, and are not satisfied when they have them. They always want a little more liberty than white men, and if they can't get it they fancy themselves ill treated.... Acting upon the mistaken notion that freedom is without limits, they succeed in making themselves hated wherever they go.... Who, then, but themselves are to blame for the prejudices existing against them? They never fail to find Carys and Franklins enough to flatter them in their extravagant ideas of liberty, and to pander to them for their support, and thus they are made the tools of demagogues and the enemies of themselves."

As usual, Gibbs acted as the Black community's spokesman in rebutting Shears, and again he kept the gloves off. In a letter to the *Colonist*, he wrote: "A great deal that is hasty and intemperate in disappointed aspirants may be pardoned in the heat of the moment, but the disposition exhibited in your colums in every issue since the election, to malign and misrepresent us, has induced us to lay before the community our views.... The colored people plant themselves by the side of and to the British Constitution, and principles, the spirit and essence of which are political and religious equality; equal respect for all men in the ratio of their deportment, industry, and intelligence, without distinctions of creed or color.

"Nothing more do they seek;...but they insist that they shall be the judges, as far as their votes and influence go, how near a candidate's life has been the index of these principles. How far the articles...in which the words 'niggers' and 'slaves' dance in all the mazes of negro-hating parlance [offer] one indication of these principles, we leave to the impartial to determine."

After a detailed rebuttal of Shears's argument, Gibbs went on to deal with the charge that Victoria's Blacks were "down" on everything American: "The United States is a despotism. One out of every six of the inhabitants are forbidden by statute to learn the word of the God who made them. It is the hot-bed, the very cesspool of political corruption, and its every ruling towards us has been illiberal and unjust. This hydra-headed prejudice has pursued us to this country; and attempts to assert its supremacy through every ramification of society. This we are emphatically down upon, and when we cease to be down upon it, we are fit to be scouted from every liberty-loving community . . . it is true that scattered through the length and breadth of the United States are Americans who for sterling worth, integrity, and love of the right, regardless of complexion, cannot be excelled by any on the globe. Men whose virtues many here, who claim to be Englishmen, would do well to imitate. But these are the exceptions.... We are opposed to American rule as it affects us. We are opposed to that class of men, even if they call themselves Englishmen, who sympathize with that rule, or who can copy the vices of Americans. In a word, a man who pays so little regard to genteel orthography as to spell negro with two g's is not likely to obtain a very warm support from colored voters."

The "Police Court" column was placed directly beneath Gibbs's letter; it contained reports on three cases involving Blacks. One Black man was suing the saloon-keeper J.D. Carroll for extortion after being charged fifty cents for a glass of ale; another Black was fined "for illegally detaining a dog, not *his* dog," and a third was fined "for assaulting and severely beating Patrick McTurner." Such accounts, given prominence, were obviously intended to neutralize Gibbs's arguments and to appeal to white prejudice.

Not content to wage war in his paper, De Cosmos appealed to Governor Douglas to investigate the election, and to make the poll books public. Douglas refused, saying it would be up to the new

Assembly to decide. De Cosmos then applied to the courts for a writ of mandamus to compel the governor to release the poll books, but again was turned down. "The court was astonished," wrote the judge, "when it was proposed to compel the Governor of the Colony," who was in effect the representative of the Crown.

The editorial page of the *Colonist* now began to coruscate with rage; but De Cosmos seemed to forget his earlier identification of the governing clique as the chief culprits. Now he turned his rhetoric against the Blacks alone: "a lowborn, secretly banded, prejudiced race of aliens.... Englishmen should be slaves to escaped slaves.... The fraud was committed by a degraded race, who are banded together — who can never amalgamate with us — ignorant of self-government, of British institutions — some of whose backs show the marks of the lash of slavery...."

Douglas put off examination of the poll books by the election committee for six months; the committee, in turn, refused to make them public. Its decision was an obvious attempt to maintain the cover-up, and it worked for nine more months, until March 1861. Only then did public pressure force the calling of a Court of Revision.

M.W.T. Drake was the Revising Barrister; George E. Nias was the chief objector. Some of the Blacks fought the objections on technicalities, including proper notice to appear at the court. Nias's objection to Gibbs was turned down on the grounds that it could not be proven he had been so notified. When Gibbs's partner, Peter Lester, was called to testify on his own behalf, however, he found he had played right into Nias's hands. His testimony was reported at length in the *Colonist:*

"Nias — Is that your handwriting on this paper?

"Lester — Read it, so all can hear, and then I'll tell you.

"Lester refusing to acknowledge the writing, Mr. Nias stated that he would read it for him, and read as follows:

"George E. Nias, you can hand this notice back to your masters, whose lickspittle you are. Tell them that Peter Lester has no use for waste paper. [Sensation] This (continued Mr. Nias) was written on the back of Lester's notice, and returned to me. This does not seem to qualify him for the thing he is seeking — a vote."

When Drake handed down his decision a few days later, Peter Lester and most of the other Black voters were declared disqualified.

"We held them to be aliens," De Cosmos crowed; "Treated them as such; warned them of the consequences of being made the tools of Cary & Co.; and after sixteen months from the time of our first warning they are told their sorrow, by the very same party who deceived them, that their votes are illegal."

The crusading editor's triumph was not total, for Selim Franklin somehow managed to retain his seat in the Assembly until it was dissolved in 1863. De Cosmos therefore ran in a by-election in nearby Esquimalt. Once more, the resourcefulness of the Douglas faction was tested.

The incumbent, George Tomline Gordon, had been appointed Colonial Treasurer, and was therefore obliged by custom to resign his seat and run again for election. The co-respondent in a messy British divorce case, Gordon had come to Vancouver Island under something of a cloud. But he was politically adroit, and argued that De Cosmos's name change had no validity outside California. His opponent was therefore forced to run as "William Alexander Smith, commonly known as Amor De Cosmos." Gordon's supporters spread rumors about the reasons for this name change and generally did their best to alarm Esquimalt's 26 voters.

When the polls were about to close on election day, ten had voted for Gordon and ten for "William Alexander Smith, commonly known as Amor De Cosmos." No trace could be found of the other six voters until a man named Moore was escorted in by one of De Cosmos's supporters. When the sheriff asked him which candidate he wished to vote for, Moore replied, "Amor De Cosmos."

The sheriff at once declared the poll closed; he then announced to the crowd of onlookers that he found ten votes for George Tomline Gordon, ten votes for William Alexander Smith, commonly known as Amor De Cosmos, and one vote for Amor De Cosmos. Since there was tie between two of the candidates, the sheriff said, he would have to vote to break the tie. "I vote for George Tomline Gordon."

Predictably outraged, De Cosmos again petitioned the Assembly, and yet another election committee took up the matter. It declared the election null and void because the 1859 voters' list had been used instead of that for 1860. Dr. Helmcken, as Speaker of the House, rejected the committee's report on a technicality, whereupon Gordon magnanimously resigned and ran once more. The 1859 list was again used, and he was once more elected.

The Douglas faction might well have fared better with De Cosmos after all, for Gordon was arrested in 1862 for embezzling government funds. During the investigation that followed, it was discovered that he had not even been qualified to run for the Assembly — Attorney General Cary had merely loaned him the necessary land. Cary then botched the indictment so badly that Gordon was granted a new trial. Free until then, he promptly decamped to the United States, where he was killed in the Civil War.

The political status of Victoria's Blacks continued to be an issue for some time after the Court of Revision declared them ineligible to have voted in the 1860 election. The government was now under pressure to draft a naturalization law for the colony, and in May of 1861 Attorney General Cary called a public meeting, at which he announced the imminent introduction of such a law: "We want an Alien Bill here," the *Colonist* reported him as saying, "and to put an end to the miserable, disjointed state of the Colony, I shall introduce one at the next session, giving aliens nearly every privilege. We can't get along prosperously unless we admit to citizenship nearly every foreign resident in the Colony."

Suddenly the meeting virtually blew up in Cary's face when a man in the audience asked: "Why did you put fifty or sixty foreigners on the voter's list last year without an Alien Bill?" This was of course a reference to the Blacks, and Cary replied: "I told Mr. Gibbs that he better put his name on the list and test the question as to whether they were entitled to vote." The audience was astounded to learn that the election had been a kind of political experiment. Gibbs himself was present, and rose to offer a different version. Cary, he said, had told him "that colored people who had no political status in any other country had a perfect right to vote here on taking an oath of allegiance."

Gibbs's statement provoked a "sensation," and when the uproar quieted Cary asked Gibbs: "Didn't I tell you that you had better put your names on the list to test the question?"

"You might have — I don't remember."

"Renewed laughter" was reported as the crowd's response.

One would very much like to know in what tone of voice Cary and Gibbs conducted this exchange. Was Gibbs actively supporting Cary's flimsy excuse, or genuinely uncertain about what had been said in a conversation almost two years earlier? In any case, it was now clear that Gibbs and the other Blacks had been used — with or without their knowledge — to steal an election. Cary as much as admitted it, and the white public now had a genuine grievance against the Blacks.

The government, however, retained enough tolerance to steal an election from a Black man just as calmly as it had from a white. In the autumn of 1861, a by-election was called for Victoria District. Jacob Francis, a Black who had spoken at the "Jollification," ran as an independent candidate. Born in England, Francis was unquestionably a British subject, and to judge from his campaign advertising he was a middle-of-the-roader. He addressed himself to the Electors of Victoria District:

"Gentlemen, — having been solicited by many of the voters of your District to come forward as a candidate for your suffrages, and as a vacancy has recently occurred, I now beg to offer myself as a candidate to represent you in the House of Assembly.

"Were I a member of the House of Assembly, I should devote all my energies in advocating wholesome laws, a liberal Incorporation Act, a Reform in the Courts of Justice and reduction of exorbitant fees; a Bill for the easy and cheap recovery of small debts, repeal of the infamous Registration of Deeds Act and a better law in its place. In short I should endeavor to have no law on the statute book that would not conduce to the safety and happiness of the country.

"I should not do, what we as a people are accused of doing — attending solely to the advancement of our own class — but I should consult the interests of the country in general, and those of the District in particular...."

Francis's candidacy seems to have been treated as a joke by most white voters. He was nominated by an English engineer, James Thorne, and seconded by saloon-keeper J.D. Carroll despite the rough treatment Carroll's bookkeeper had received at the hands of a gang of Blacks. Joseph Trutch was also nominated at the same meeting. It was objected that, since he was out of town,

Trutch would be unable to take the oath required of all candidates before the election, but his name was nevertheless allowed to stand. Dr. James Trimble also ran.

When the election was held, Trimble and Trutch won easily, with Francis a poor third. Only two of the five Blacks qualified to vote had cast their ballots for Francis, and most of his white supporters reportedly wanted to "create a row in the House of Assembly," not strike a blow for equality. But Trutch's candidacy was obviously illegal. He had not even been in the colony at the time of the election. The Victoria newspapers agreed that Francis had a legal right to take one of the two seats; as a writer in the *Daily Press* put it:

"It may be objected that he wears his necktie in a peculiar manner — that he keeps a drinking saloon — or that he did not take his degree at Oxford — but we do not think the members will find such objections valid according to Blackstone or any of the other legal authorities of Great Britain."

Determined to overthrow Trutch's election, Francis hired a lawyer and circulated a petition. Meanwhile Trimble and Trutch were sworn in and took their seats, beginning long careers in British Columbia affairs. Trutch, a civil engineer who built the Yale-Cariboo road, eventually became British Columbia's Lieutenant Governor; Trimble, a Royal Navy surgeon, would later serve as mayor of Victoria and as Speaker of the House. The Assembly appointed an election committee to consider Francis's petition; since the government had no intention of allowing a Black man into the Assembly, the committee turned down the petition on a technicality: there were "erasures and interlineations" in the document. The deadline for such petitions had now passed, and Francis was refused an extension to prepare a new version, so he was effectively shut out of the Assembly despite his legal election.

Such was the Blacks' introduction to colonial politics. "Justice" in early Victoria meant that scoundrels and hypocrites went unpunished and that some even basked in undeserved glory. There may have been some poetic justice in the fact that George Hunter Cary soon went bankrupt trying to build an enormous mansion, returned to England, and died insane at the age of 34. Amor De Cosmos, after a long career in provincial and federal politics (he was the premier of British Columbia for a year), also died insane.

Knighted in 1863, Sir James Douglas was made a Knight Commander of the Bath upon his retirement the following year. He later observed that "representative Governments cannot be carried on without recourse directly or indirectly to bribery and corrupting influences." Personally admirable but politically unscrupulous, he knew whereof he spoke.

CHAPTER SEVEN

"A most orderly and useful and loyal section of the community"

For the most part, Victoria's Blacks spent little time or energy in battling prejudice or seeking justice. They, like their white neighbors, were preoccupied with making a living, getting ahead, and minding their own business. Mifflin Gibbs, for one, soon found himself doing so well that in the spring of 1859 he left for an extended visit to the eastern United States. In Oberlin, Ohio, he mét and married a girl from Kentucky named Maria Alexander, who had studied at Oberlin from 1852 to 1854. The newlyweds visited a number of Gibbs's old comrades, including Frederick Douglass, before making the long voyage back to Victoria. In the next seven years she would bear their five children.

For all their private concerns, the Blacks were remarkably civic-minded. One of the first public projects they supported was the formation of a volunteer fire brigade. Fire fighting was not yet seen as a government service; instead, public donations financed volunteer units. Membership was prestigious, and not available just for the asking. To join a fire brigade cost a hundred dollars, but there was no lack of volunteers.

The Blacks, including the owners of some valuable and inflammable property, were generous contributors to the fund for the proposed fire brigade. In October 1859 the "Hook and Ladder Committee" met to plan the beginning of the fire fighting service. Jacob Francis was there, and, as the *Colonist* reported, he "remarked that as the French residents were represented on the Committee; and as the colored population had subscribed liberally and were largely interested in property here, he thought they should also be represented on the Committee. He therefore moved 'that two from the colored residents be added to the Committee.' "The motion was seconded by Mr. Johnson; but lost."

The whites who controlled the committee also controlled the membership of the fire brigade and blackballed any volunteers they disliked. No Black — although several volunteered — was accepted.

The Blacks then approached Governor Douglas with a proposal to form a volunteer militia unit. The idea had been in the air for some time; such units were then fashionable in Britain because of fears of a French invasion. In the colony of Vancouver Island a similar war scare was developing — the so-called "Pig War" over control of San Juan Island. Claimed by Britain and used as a Hudson's Bay Company farm, the island had been occupied by U.S. troops under General Harney after an American settler shot a British pig. Harney was acting without orders, and seems to have seriously embarrassed the U.S. government by his action. In one of his few misjudgements, Douglas had ordered the British naval forces at Esquimalt to take the island back. The officers stalled him until their commander, Admiral Baynes, returned to port. Baynes very sensibly refused to embroil Britain in almost certain war with the United States.

The dispute was to go on for over a decade, but in its first few months it looked very serious. The British colonists were reminded of their vulnerability; the Americans in Victoria saw a chance to annex Vancouver Island and British Columbia to the United States. In addition, there were growing fears of an Indian war, in which the colonists would be seriously outnumbered.

Douglas was as always short of funds, so the Blacks' idea of a self-supporting volunteer unit was attractive. He gave his assent, and recruiting started at once. By the spring of 1860, between forty and fifty Black men were enrolled in the Victoria Pioneer Rifle Company. The corps was not officially sworn in until July of 1861, but by that time it was already a well known and popular organization. None of its members had previous military experience, but the navy supplied drill sergeants from its vessels. The volunteers built a drill hall on Yates Street which soon became a social center for the whole Black community. In good weather, the corps drilled on Beacon Hill, overlooking the Strait of Juan de Fuca and the mountains of the Olympic Peninsula. Their uniforms, ordered from England, were green with orange facings; judging from a photograph of the unit taken in 1864, it looked as soldierly as any company in the U.S. Civil War.

The volunteers' arms were a continuing problem, however. They relied on archaic flintlocks, borrowed from the Hudson's Bay Company, which were little better than broomsticks. Douglas asked the Colonial Office for adequate weapons, and in the spring of 1862 he received 29 cases of rifles and 250 barrels of ammunition; a little later, 500 more rifles arrived. Evidently none of these reached the Black militia, for its officers were still asking for them in 1864.

The VPRC (also known as the African Rifles) was nevertheless glamorous enough to attract a number of applications from white volunteers. These were rejected, giving the Blacks the sour consolation of revenge. Perhaps as a result of these rejections, a white militia unit also came into being in the summer of 1861. The Vancouver Island Volunteer Rifle Corps vanished within a few months because of internal squabbles. The African Rifles, by contrast, seem to have conducted their affairs harmoniously, and to have enjoyed considerable community support. They held dances and entertainments in their drill hall to raise money, and sometimes received donations from the Black women of Victoria. This income was not enough to maintain the unit, but the volunteers managed to delay asking for government help until late in 1861. Learning that $1,250 had been budgeted for "the different Volunteers corps of the colony," Captain Fortune Richard applied to the governor "for such portion of that sum as his excellency shall think fit to allow us." Douglas ordered $250 to be paid to the African Rifles.

One wonders what became of the remaining thousand dollars; certainly there were no other units to claim it, as was shown by Douglas's 1862 report on the colony's military forces. The Blacks felt they deserved it, and later in the year they applied for it, citing the need to expand and improve their drill hall. Nothing came of this request, or of later ones, but somehow the corps managed to survive for several years and even to form the Victoria City Brass Band as an auxiliary.

The officers and men of the African Rifles took considerable
pride in their unit. During the 1861 visit of Lady Jane Franklin,
a delegation from the volunteers paid a call on the famous widow.
Sophia Cracroft, Lady Franklin's niece and traveling companion,
recorded the meeting in a letter home:

"At 5 o'clock the Bishop [George Hills] came to be present at
the visits of the coloured people who had asked my Aunt to see
them...The first was Mr. Gibbs, a most respectable merchant who
is rising fast. His manner is exceedingly good, & his way of speaking quite refined. He is not quite black, but his hair is I believe
short & crisp. Three other men arrived after him & he took his
leave soon after, having acted rather as spokesman for the others,
who then explained that they were the Captain & other officers of
a Coloured Rifle Corps, & the Captain proceeded to speak very
feelingly of the prejudices existing here even, against their colour.
He said they knew it was because of the strong American element
which entered into the community, which however they hoped
one day to see overpowered by the English one; — that they had
come here hoping to find that true freedom which could be enjoyed only under English privileges, & great had been their disappointment to find that their origin was against them.

"My Aunt sympathised with them of course, & said she knew
their claims had been always maintained by the Bishop as representing the Church. This observation was eagerly taken up by
the Lieut who said that but for the stand made on their behalf
by the Bishop & his clergy, the coloured population would have
left the colony in a body. We shd thus have lost a most orderly
and useful and loyal section of the community. They naturally
detest America, & this Rifle corps has been formed by them *really*
with the view of resisting any American aggression, such as this San
Juan alarm, still pending.

"As he went out, the Captain said 'Depend upon it, Madam, if
Uncle Sam goes too far, we shall be able to give a good account of
ourselves.' You can imagine how gratified the Bishop was by this
emphatic declaration of their obligations to himself & his clergy."

It is uncertain how serious the officer was in claiming that the
Blacks had nearly left Victoria over the church dispute; no indication of such an attitude reached the newspapers. And while the

morale of the volunteers was no doubt high at this time, it is unlikely that forty or fifty ill-equipped militiamen could have resisted
American professional soldiers.

Sophia Cracroft's letter also noted other interesting aspects of
Victoria's Black community. She and Lady Franklin arrived in
early March and found more than adequate lodging in the home
of Wellington Moses—"the very best in the place & really *very*
tolerable—a tidy little sitting room & bedroom behind for my
Aunt—the landlady giving up her own room (above) for me."

Moses, born in England, had had an earlier connection with
the Arctic explorer Sir John Franklin, as Sophia Cracroft remarked:
"He was very nearly going out with my dear Uncle—only his wife
at last refused to let him go. [This must have been another wife,
for Moses had married Sarah Jane Douglas in Victoria in December of 1858.] They are very respectable people. He is a hair cutter
& has a shop—the naval people especially patronize him...& his
wife has the reputation of being a first rate cook...Mr. Moses calls
himself an Englishman, which of course he is politically & therefore justly. She is a queer being, wears a long sweeping gown without crinoline—moves slowly & has a sort of stately way (in intention at least) which is quite amusing. Sometimes she ties a coloured
handkerchief around her head like the American negroes (she is
from Baltimore)....The language of both is very good. Mr. Moses
said to Captn Richards when he was arranging about our being
taken in, 'The fact is Sir, my wife is the best housekeeper in the
country except yours.' Captn Richards begged he wd make no
exception in favour of Mrs. R. who he was sure cd not equal Mrs.
Moses!"

The English ladies toured the colony's schools, and were again
reminded of the recent church dispute. Some whites had pressured
Bishop Hills to segregate the church schools, "but the Bishop was
not likely to give way upon such a point, and his firmness met
with its reward—the threatened withdrawal of the other students
never took place, and we saw the unmistakable descendants of
negroes, in Mrs. Woods' little school of 30, side by side with the
English and American girls. The struggle has not been very long
past, & at one time seemed serious."

Sophia Cracroft's observations show what seems to have been a typical upper-class English ambivalence toward the Blacks: an indignant distaste for American prejudice, coupled with almost obsessive remarks about the Blacks' appearance — complexion, hair texture, voice, and manner.

Though American whites periodically agitated for school segregation in Victoria, they got nowhere. Blacks and whites attended classes together, and in general got along well. Edgar Fawcett, who came to Victoria as a boy with his parents, later recalled a fight between a Black pupil and a white one: "I was mainly instrumental in bringing it about," he wrote in his reminiscences, "and backed my man until the sponge was thrown up by the white boy's friend." There seems to have been no racial motive to the fight, just juvenile bloody-mindedness. Fawcett was severely punished when his role in the fight came out, and he observed ruefully: "I got little sympathy at home when I told them I had been whipped for causing a fight between a white boy and a black boy named White."

For all the discrimination they met, Victoria's Blacks could rely on the law to protect their interests more effectively than it ever had in California. One dramatic proof of this occurred in September 1860, when the Black community learned that a runaway slave was being held aboard the American mail steamer *Eliza Anderson,* then in Victoria harbor. The slave, a boy named Charles Mitchell, had run away from Major James Tilton of Olympia, Washington Territory. On September 24 he had stowed away on the steamer just before it left Olympia for Vancouver Island. He was discovered en route, and the vessel's captain, John Fleming, had him locked up in a cabin. Fleming planned to keep him there until the ship returned to Olympia, but somehow word got out to the Blacks in Victoria. They immediately went to Attorney General Cary, who drew up affidavits and applied to Chief Justice Cameron for a writ of habeas corpus. The writ was directed to Sheriff Naylor, who was thus empowered to take Charles Mitchell into custody and bring him before the court.

Sheriff Naylor went down to the waterfront, just a few yards from the government buildings, and went aboard the *Eliza Ander-*

son to demand the boy. Captain Fleming at first refused, though he knew he might be putting himself in trouble with the colonial authorities. But he also had to go home to Washington Territory, where Major Tilton awaited the return of his slave. Unimpressed, Sheriff Naylor said he would break down the door of Charles's cabin if it were not opened. Since Naylor was an enormous man who looked as if he could do the job single-handedly, Fleming gave in.

Sheriff, slave, and sea captain now came ashore, and went directly to Chief Justice Cameron's court, where Cary waited to act as Charles's counsel. After reading the affidavits the Blacks had signed, Cary argued that British authorities had every right to board a foreign vessel in a British port and to take Charles out of unlawful custody. In any case, Cary went on, the mere presence of Charles Mitchell on British soil made him *ipso facto* a free man. His precedent was the 1772 case of Somersett vs. Steuart, in which Lord Mansfield had held that any slave touching British soil became free by so doing.

Captain Fleming found legal counsel as swiftly as Charles had, and with the help of attorney George Pearkes he composed and filed a protest against the sheriff — more likely to cover himself with his neighbors in Olympia than to influence Chief Justice Cameron: "...the said Sheriff threatened to force open the room in which the Negro was confined on board of said vessel Whereupon the undersigned to prevent the destruction of property and in all probability much bloodshed opened the door of said room and upon doing so the Sheriff took the Negro from on board said vessel.

"Now therefore the undersigned protests against the whole proceedings as illegal and a breach of international law, and demands the immediate delivery of the said negro Charles that he may be returned to his master."

Cameron took little time to rule that Charles Mitchell should be set free, and was applauded by the audience. On the same day he had arrived a prisoner, Charles Mitchell found himself free; to Victoria's Blacks, it must have been exhilarating to win so swift a legal triumph after the endless delays of the Archy Lee case back in California.

While at least one Washington Territory newspaper protested Cameron's decision, sentiment in Victoria was generally favorable. Amor De Cosmos relaxed his anti-Black campaign long enough to gibe at American hypocrisy; he also noted that since Victoria was a free port, "not even negroes can be kept *in bond* here."

Charles Mitchell was soon enrolled in the Boys' Collegiate School run by the Anglicans in the same "upper-room" Reverend Clarke had used during his short ministry. Here, six months later, he came to the attention of Sophia Cracroft, who mentioned in passing that his "history excited a good deal of attention in these parts.... He is not particularly intelligent." What her evidence might have been is unknown, but, intelligent or not, Charles Mitchell was free — and a witness that even a crooked government could sometimes do the right thing.

When Blacks themselves came in conflict with the colony's laws, it was generally for trivial reasons, and they were treated as fairly as their white neighbors. A typical case came before the courts late in the summer of 1860. Under the heading "A Rumpus Among the Negroes," the *Colonist* reported it at length, probably because it involved a racially mixed couple and had a good deal of humorous human interest.

"Yesterday morning Timothy Roberts, a negro drayman, appeared in court to answer a charge of using disgusting language towards a buxom negress, named Elizabeth Leonard. Roberts came into court with his wife, a diminutive Irishwoman, who stood by her husband's side during the investigation, and prompted him occasionally as he made his defence.

"Mrs. Leonard said that last Sunday morning some of her chickens got over into Roberts' yard, and that R. wrung their necks, and used insulting language, calling her a 'black —' etc.

"A witness, called to substantiate Mrs. L., testified that she saw Roberts twist the necks of the chickens, and Mrs. Leonard said to him, 'That is an unliberal, unchristianized act.' Roberts said, 'Git out, you black —,' and told her do something vulgar.

"The Judge asked Roberts what he had to say for himself?

"*Roberts* — You see, Judge, this 'ere woman, and all the other colored folks, is down on my wife because she's Irish. I can't help it because she's Irish—'tain't my fault. (Sensation in court, and slight hissing.) They calls my wife Irish, and keeps a using insulting language towards her whenever she goes in the yard, and says I'm a nadgy-headed nigger.

"*Mrs. Roberts*—Your honor, I want pertection; but I suppose I must put up with undecent remarks because I lives in a low neighborhood. I am rebuked and reviled every time I go into the yard.

"*The Judge*—Well, Roberts, you will have to find two sureties in 20 pounds sterling each to be of good behavior in future, or in default suffer one month's imprisonment.

"The negro, closely followed by his white wife, was then led off to prison, grumbling at his hard streak of luck. We learn that he afterwards furnished the bonds and was set at liberty."

Racial tension was also involved in another case, when a Black teamster named Stephen Farrington charged three whites with assaulting him. One of the three, John Guest, was a notorious troublemaker who had been in numerous scrapes before. "The complainant swore that he had been called a very bad name by Mr. John Parker while on his way to Esquimalt with his team to meet the steamer, because he could not turn out and let Parker pass; that when they had all reached Esquimalt he went to Parker and remonstrated with him for his language, whereupon [Thomas] Burnes struck and knocked him down and Guest and [William] Bough kicked him while he lay on the ground. As a proof...witness exhibited a black eye. He also swore that he was sober at the time of the row.

"Several witnesses were called to prove that the complainant was drunk and abusive to the whites; that Guest only struck after being assailed with a black-snake in the hands of a colored teamster; that Burnes, while the fight was progressing...remained a passive spectator, and that Bough was a long distance away...

"Solomon Stevens (colored) called as a witness for the prosecution, was proved to have been very abusive and in company with his friend Farrington behaved so outrageously and made so much noise as to cause Chief Justice Cameron, who chanced to be on the spot, to send a messenger to Victoria for a policeman. Mr. Pemberton accordingly dismissed the case against all the accused."

Such incidents were to be expected among teamsters and others accustomed to solving problems with their fists. But the Black man who seemed to get into the most trouble with the law was a solid middle-class entrepreneur named Willis Bond. Born a slave in Tennessee in 1824, Bond had entered California as a "servant" and had earned enough to buy his freedom. He reached Victoria in the first days of the gold rush and went on to Yale, where he and an English partner supplied water for mining operations. A few months later he returned to Victoria and began running a number of enterprises.

Bond's first brush with the law was in early 1859, when he was charged with selling unwholesome food and counterfeiting flour brands. He was found not guilty, but a few years later he found himself in court again and again: he failed to pay an employee's wages, he got into fistfights on the street, he wrecked a neighbor's fence, and he once obstructed Government Street for three days with a house he was moving.

For all his legal problems, Bond was better known as an orator, and even built a lecture room as an annex to a bar he owned. In this "Athenaeum Room," he spoke on politics, economics, and race, and sometimes debated issues with local celebrities. Bond's speeches were lively, well attended events, but they occasionally got out of hand. On one occasion, he spoke against giving a government subsidy to the Mechanics' Institute, which refused membership to Blacks. Someone in the large crowd of listeners threw pepper on the stove, driving the audience upstairs. Bond refused to leave, however, even though someone tossed a string of firecrackers into the room. His audience finally returned, but was again dispersed with pepper and firecrackers.

Over a century later, most of the quarrels and annoyances that beset Victoria's Blacks in the early 1860s seem comfortingly trivial: a few brawls, a few teapot tempests played for laughs by the newspapers of the time. Of course these incidents provoked genuine sorrow, anger, or triumph among the Blacks, but they did not poison the whole community's atmosphere as later events would.

It is also worth noting that most of the anti-Black feeling in the British Northwest was confined to the muddy streets of Victoria. In the gold fields of the Cariboo and on Saltspring Island, Blacks and whites lived and worked together with little friction. They had their sorrows and misfortunes, but racism was not one of them.

CHAPTER EIGHT

"Have we any rights in common
with white men?"

L ate in June 1858, an Indian canoe was found drifting down
the Fraser, not far from the river's mouth. In it was a Black man
near death from seven stab wounds. He was the second cook of
the small steamship *Sea Bird,* which had been carrying miners up
the Fraser when it struck a sandbar near Yale. Her passengers had
continued on foot while the crew decided what to do next. Some
chose to stay; others, including the cook, hired local Indians to
take them back downriver. The cook had been the only passenger
in his canoe, and when the party camped overnight he was stabbed
and robbed. Somehow he managed to escape in the canoe, but
was too seriously wounded to do anything but let the current take
him. Taken to hospital in Victoria, he died within a day or two,
probably the first Black casualty of the gold rush.

The route to the gold fields was dangerous enough in itself.
From Victoria, thousands of men crossed the Strait of Georgia in
canoes, rowboats — anything that would float. Once on the mainland, they could either walk the hundred miles to Fort Hope or
labor upriver against a strong current. At Yale, a few miles north
of Fort Hope, the Fraser Canyon narrowed the river to a turbulent
ribbon of white water. "About one-fourth of the canoes that attempt to come up are lost in the rapids," one early prospector
noted. Governor Douglas himself, in May 1858, reported to London
that "many accidents have happened in the dangerous rapids of
that river; a great number of canoes having been dashed to pieces
and their cargoes swept away by the impetuous stream, while of

the ill-fated adventurers who accompanied them, many have been swept into eternity." This was the fate of a Black, nine Chinese, and a white man in November 1860, in a mishap at China Bar Riffle from which only one man — another Black — escaped alive.

The alternative to the river passage was scarcely safer: to creep along narrow trails on the steep slopes of the canyon, with a long drop to the rocks and rapids below. "We had to pass where no human being should venture," Simon Fraser wrote of the canyon route in 1806, and it was no better fifty years later.

Faced with these hazards, the miners welcomed Douglas's 1858 project to build a road bypassing the worst of the trip. Several hundred miners, including some Blacks, built the road from Harrison Lake to Lillooet for only the cost of their food. These were no small wages; poor transport meant staggering costs for supplies in the interior. Beef was twenty cents a pound in Victoria, but a dollar a pound on the Fraser, while fifty cents' worth of tobacco in Victoria brought six dollars in the gold country. The new road helped to bring down prices very quickly.

The local Indians were also a problem. Predictably alarmed at the invasion of thousands of strangers, they began to pick off the miners one by one. A bloody Indian war was then being fought in Washington Territory, and news of the battles no doubt aggravated matters on the Fraser; so did the arrogance of the Americans, the "Boston men," who had never been trusted as "King George's men" were. By midsummer of 1858, conflict with the Indians had become critical. Several bodies had floated down the Fraser to Yale, and twenty-two out of twenty-six in one party had been killed in a running battle through the canyon.

Determined not to let matters get out of hand, Douglas himself led a party of British sailors up the river. He soon found, however, that the miners had already dealt with the problem; several hundred of them, heavily armed, had marched up the Fraser in a show of force, and had then concluded peace treaties with the Indians. The implications of their action were quite as serious as the Indians' hostility, so Douglas seized the opportunity to assert the Crown's authority over "the motley population of foreigners now assembled on the Fraser" by setting up a court at Fort Hope to try a miner charged with murder. After the trial he spoke to a gathering of three thousand miners, and later reported that they gave "three cheers for the Queen, but evidently with a bad grace. There is a strong American feeling among them, and they will require constant watching until the English element preponderates in the colony."

Douglas especially disliked the Americans' readiness to take the law into their own hands. He therefore appointed a number of "Stipendiary Magistrates" — all British subjects — to keep order in the mining camps. These men acted as the local gold and lands commissioners, tax collectors, and even coroners; none had any legal training. Each, however, was jealous of his authority, and when two of them came into conflict in the winter of 1858-59, the result was a small war. No shot was fired: it was a comic-opera affair, though serious — like the Pig War — in its overtones.

The episode began on Christmas Day 1858, when an American miner named Farrell walked from his claim at Hill's Bar to Yale, a mile or so upriver. There he got drunk and pistol-whipped a Black barber named Isaac Dickson. Farrell then lurched back to Hill's Bar, while Dickson lodged a complaint with Mr. Whannell, the Yale magistrate. Whannell issued a warrant for Farrell's arrest and sent it to Hill's Bar to be served on the miner. Hill's Bar had its own magistrate, a man named George Perrier, who resented this invasion of his domain. He issued his own warrant — for Dickson's arrest. Perrier's constable tried to apprehend the Black man right in Whannell's court; Whannell promptly put the constable in jail on a charge of contempt of court.

Perrier now issued a warrant for the arrest of Whannell, and this time it was served by a whole posse whose leader was an American named Ned McGowan. McGowan had been in serious trouble with the San Francisco Vigilance Committee for his role in a murder (he had even been shot at as he boarded ship for the gold fields). Annoyed by the squabble between the two magistrates, McGowan took Perrier's side and marched into Yale. He freed the Hill's Bar constable, invaded Whannell's court, and arrested him. The furious magistrate was bundled into a canoe and taken downriver to Perrier, who fined his colleague fifty dollars for contempt of court.

McGowan was now the real authority in Hill's Bar, and took advantage of his position to beat up a man who had been with the vigilantes in San Francisco. British miners on the Fraser were alarmed at these events, and sent semi-hysterical reports to Victoria: "Yankee Rowdies defying the law! Every peaceable citizen frightened out of his wits! Summons and warrants laughed to scorn!"

Douglas promptly sent HMS *Plumper*, armed with a small howitzer, up the Fraser to restore order. Aboard were Col. Richard Clement Moody with a company of his Royal Engineers; a hundred sailors; and British Columbia's first judge, Matthew Baillie Begbie. The arrival of this force was a turning point. Had Douglas not acted decisively, McGowan might have turned his comic revolt into a genuine takeover and become the *de facto* ruler of the gold fields.

While most of the party halted at Langley, Colonel Moody and his engineers entered Yale. He was greeted by a mob of American miners who fired their revolvers over his head. "If it was to try my nerves," he later wrote, "they must have forgotten my profession. I stood up, and raised my cap and thanked them in the Queen's name for their loyal reception of me."

Finding the urbane colonel unintimidated, the miners relaxed somewhat, and Ned McGowan decided to give himself up. He and his followers must have realized that they were trapped by geography as much as by Moody's soldiers. Surrounded by range after range of mountains, the Fraser canyon offers no easy exit except the river itself. With a determined government in control of the Fraser's lower reaches, the miners were bottled up.

A day or two later, Judge Begbie arrived. He was much like his patron, Douglas: big, arrogant, and sometimes self-dramatizing. As a lawyer in England, Begbie had had indifferent success; now, at 39, he was in his true element for the first time. With his Van Dyke beard, his penetrating glare, and his judicial robes and wig, Begbie made a powerful impression on the rebel miners. He fired Perrier and his constable, reinstated Whannell, and fined McGowan heavily. McGowan responded by inviting the judge home for a drink, which Begbie was glad to accept. The two men then toured the diggings, on the very best of terms. Despite this cordial conclusion to "Ned McGowan's War," the government felt it had proved, as Moody put it, that "in the Queen's dominions an infringement of the Law was really a serious matter, and not a sort of half joke as in California."

For years thereafter, Judge Begbie went on demonstrating that any infringement of his concept of "the Law" was serious indeed. He gained a reputation as "the hanging judge," but more from his fiery rhetoric than from his sentences. In one of his most celebrated eruptions, he chastised a jury for bringing in a verdict of manslaughter when premeditated murder had been proven: "You, gentlemen of the jury, you are a pack of Dalles horse thieves, and permit me to say it would give me the greatest pleasure to see you hanged, each and every one of you, for declaring a murderer guilty only of manslaughter." In another murder case, the accused was found not guilty, prompting an earnest appeal from Begbie: "The jury in their infinite wisdom have declared that you are not guilty of sandbagging the deceased. In return for this I would simply state that you would do me an inestimable favour if, after leaving the court house, you sandbag each and every one of that jury, and see that not one escapes.... You can go."

Few juries risked Begbie's displeasure, however, and he generally ran his court as he pleased. While he allowed American lawyers to represent their countrymen, Begbie refused to allow Canadian-trained lawyers to argue their cases before him. (This may have been a personal idiosyncrasy, but it no doubt appealed to many English miners, who called the Canadians "North American Chinamen.") Begbie's word was indeed law, and the colonial government gave him complete freedom.

The miners moved steadily up the Fraser in 1859 and 1860 and began to fan out into the river's tributaries. They were convinced that somewhere lay a rich lode, the source of the fine gold that had been washed downriver. In 1861, a party of miners discovered it on Williams Creek, in the Cariboo country east of the Fraser. A new rush started at once, and Black men took an active part in it. Before long, Williams Creek was the site of a string of mining towns, including Richfield, which became the administrative center of the Cariboo, and Barkerville, which for a time was the largest town west of Chicago and north of San Francisco.

Mining here was no simple matter of gold pans and sluice boxes. The gold of Williams Creek was usually well below the surface, so that shafts had to be dug and pumped dry. Since individuals could not meet the enormous capital costs of shaft mining, they formed scores of companies to exploit the new bonanza. Some of these companies were made up partly or entirely of Blacks; one such group, though inexperienced, made twenty to forty dollars a day on Horsefly Creek in 1863. Other Blacks prospered in supplying the miners' needs: they included William Jones, an Oberlin graduate who was one of Barkerville's first dentists; the caretaker of the Barkerville Court House; a restaurant owner named Steele; and Isaac Dickson, who had moved upriver from Yale. A reasonably large Black population is suggested by the fact that *The Elevator,* a Black newspaper published in San Francisco, had a Barkerville correspondent and distributed copies in the Cariboo.

As in Victoria, few of the Black pioneers in the Cariboo were involved in serious crime. A Black named William Laura was stabbed to death in the Fraser Canyon in 1860, but there seem to have been few other cases of violent crime in which Blacks were involved. In the summer of 1863, when Judge Begbie made one of his regular sweeps through the region, holding court on horseback or in tents, he reported with self-satisfaction: "There has not been a single crime of violence committed in the Cariboo since my arrival in June last — till three days ago, when one nigger was so insulted by an allusion to the fact of his day before yesterday's breakfast being unpaid for, that he drew a knife and made two or three desperate stabs at the waiter (also a nigger). The plaintiff and defendant were both among the blackest men you could see. The rascal might have committed murder — manslaughter at least — but luckily the waiter was the stronger of the two, and when the prisoner saw the blood flowing pretty freely he got frightened & tried to escape. It was the only case of stabbing that has occurred. The jury might very well have found a felonious intent which would have given him 10 to 15 years. They took the lighter view of the matter however — so I gave him 3 years. — He is a good cook I believe, & [Chief Inspector of Police] Brew will find him useful at New Westminster in that capacity."

Sometime in the mid-1860s, Wellington Moses arrived in the Cariboo. His marital problems may have been the cause of his leaving Victoria: his wife (whose somewhat odd appearance and manner had been noted by Sophia Cracroft) had attempted to drown herself in Victoria harbor in 1862. When rescued, she had claimed that her husband had left her for another woman.

If he did, however, Moses' diaries never mention the fact. After wandering up and down the Fraser for a few years, he settled in Barkerville. Here he ran a sort of barbershop and dry goods store, selling everything from ladies' shoes ("No more cold feet!" his ads promised) to his own Hair Invigorator, which he advertised in both the Cariboo and Victoria papers: "TO PREVENT BALDNESS, restore hair that has fallen off or become thin, and to cure effectually Scurf or Dandruff. It will also relieve the Headache, and give the hair a darker and glossy color, and the free use of it will keep both the skin and hair in a healthy state. Ladies will find the Invigorator a great addition to toilet, both in consideration of the agreeable and delicate perfume, and the great facility it affords in dressing the hair.... When used on children's heads, it lays the foundation for a good head of hair." Although a single treatment with the Invigorator cost $25, he had a steady stream of customers for it, and some offered testimonials to its effectiveness in curing baldness.

Like most of the Blacks in the gold country, Moses led a quiet, uneventful life; most of his diary entries are concerned with the weather or his financial accounts. On one occasion, however, he helped to send a man to the gallows for murder.

In the spring of 1866, Moses had traveled south to New Westminster, and on his return late in May he became the traveling companion of a young Bostonian named Charles Morgan Blessing. Leaving their steamer at Yale, the two men continued north on foot toward Barkerville. At Quesnelmouth, they encountered another man, James Barry, who was also looking for company. Moses planned to break his journey for a few days; Blessing, however, was impatient to go on. As Moses later testified, Blessing was a timid man who distrusted most people, and he had reservations about Barry. And, although he had only fifty or sixty dollars, Blessing was afraid of being robbed. His appearance may have made him seem more prosperous than he was: he sported an unusual tiepin, with a gold nugget naturally shaped like a man's profile. Overcoming his fears, Blessing left with Barry after agreeing to meet Moses at Van Winkle, a mining camp on the road to Barkerville. When Moses reached Van Winkle, he found no sign of Blessing, and went on to Barkerville. A few days later he met Barry in the street.

"What have you done with my chummy?" Moses asked.

"Who? Oh, that coon. [Since Blessing was white, it was an odd term for him.] I have not seen him since the morning we left the Mouth. I left him on the road. He could not travel; he had a sore foot."

Moses saw Barry twice more in following days, and each time asked about Blessing; the third time, Barry "looked savagely" at him, and muttered something under his breath.

One day in October, Moses was shaving a customer and noticed the man's tie pin. It was obviously Blessing's; there was no mistaking the nugget with the man's profile.

"Where did you get that?" the barber asked.

"From a hurdie," the man replied. The hurdy-gurdy girls of the Cariboo dance halls were understandably popular in a country with few women; Moses in turn was popular with them, since he stocked ladies' clothing and perfume, and often loaned the girls money. He soon found the hurdie, who told him James Barry had given her the pin some time ago.

Now alarmed and suspicious, Moses went to Judge Cox in nearby Richfield. By coincidence, a report had just come in about the discovery of Blessing's body, not far from where he and Barry had last been seen together. Blessing had been shot once, in the back of the head, and his body had been concealed in dense bush some forty yards below the trail. As soon as news of the murder became public, Barry disappeared. On the strength of Moses' information, Judge Cox sent Constable John Sullivan out to track him down.

Sullivan knew that Barry was surely heading south, and rode cross-country to try to intercept him at Soda Creek. He was too late: Barry had caught the stagecoach from Soda Creek to Yale. Had he left a day or two earlier, Barry would almost surely have escaped, but as it happened the telegraph line from New Westminster had just been completed as far as Soda Creek. Sullivan sent the first message south, describing Barry to the authorities at Yale. When they took him off the stage, Barry gave a false name at first; undeceived, the local constable sent him back north. When Sullivan took custody of the fugitive, Barry asked what he was charged with, and who had laid the charge. Sullivan replied that he would be told the details when they reached Richfield.

"It is the colored man, Moses the barber," Barry said. "He was always asking me what had become of a man who had come up with me, and at last I got vexed and told him, 'I was no caretaker of that man.'"

Barry was kept in jail until the next assizes, in July 1867. Judge Begbie heard the case, including the testimony of Wellington Moses. Though all the evidence was circumstantial, there was certainly enough to convict, and the jury took only an hour to find Barry guilty. Asked if he had anything to say before sentence was passed, Barry began an incoherent story about leaving Blessing with a stranger while he himself went on with a party of Chinese. Then, as if realizing it was futile, he broke off in mid-sentence. As Begbie concluded in his report of the trial, "Sentence of death was then passed in the usual way."

Barry's death warrant, with its official seal pressed into black wax, was issued on July 16. Three weeks later, he was hanged at Richfield. Moses, meanwhile, had taken up a collection to give Charles Morgan Blessing a proper funeral and to put a headstone and railing on the young man's grave.

Most of the Blacks in the Barkerville area were far less prominent than Moses, but Isaac Dickson—veteran of Ned McGowan's War—enjoyed considerable popularity. "Dixie" had a quick sense of humor, and in the columns of the *Cariboo Sentinel* he used dialect to poke fun at life in the gold fields. In our own genteel era, dialect humor has unpleasant overtones of Stepin Fetchit, but a century ago it was an accepted means of mixing laughter and social criticism. Isaac Dickson showed talent in the form.

In the first of his two letters, Dixie opened with his compliments to the editor and his hopes for the newspaper's success: "It gibs me much pleasure indee to see genelman ob your cloth on Williams Creek dis air season, an' hope, sar, de indefatable entarprice an' de talen I sees 'splayed in de columbs ob yer valable jernal will meet wid its juss rewad, dat is, dat de paper will pay big;...take de culed fren's adwice 'bout looking arter No. 1."

The barber went on to comment on Barkerville's professional gamblers: "De genelman dat goes round all de day wid hans in de pocket an' puts on de frills, dont know how him lib, yet peers to get all de fat bones to pick, so, some folks say him lib on BOOKS, on DECK, if dats de case him awful vegtarian, an' grate charity of Capin Cox to change him diet, an' sen him below."

Dixie offered the editor some advice on "de style of pugilistickism is dis counry" — "if eber you get in a muss, mister editer, neber tink to get out ob it on de squarr, if yer do yer gon in shure, pick up trifle like de axe, crowbar, or anyting ob dat sort dat's not too hard...de boot bery good substute or shub de tum into de corner ob his eye, and be sure de eye cums out 'fore de tum, den when its out kick it in 'gain wid de boot, dat de style...."

The hurdy-gurdy girls came in for some praise: "Dere's de Dush gals, dey's purty smart gals, mister editer, to hold dere own in dis counry, poor gals, I hope dey may continy to do so; de stokeepers is offul down on de gals too, coss dey draw de boys, and draw de dollars; but de sloon keepers oughter know dat de dance galls aluss took better dan anyting else in Californey, de meenus man will spen a dollar for a dance, coss him 'dearly lubs de lasses, O.'"

One local resident, according to Dixie, was so foul-mouthed that he ought to "war a mustash for de durty words to wipe dere feet on...But dis genelman, like eberybody else, hab him good qualtys, an' deserbes de tanks ob de leddies for his volunery an' gratutus saveses as night watchman during pas winter; no 'voted luber eber suffed more from cowl wile singeing under winer ob his gal's chamer dan dis venable owl cuss las winer wile watchin like a teef for de hoptunity to pilfa de fair name of 'specable women.'"

The editor was understandably glad to learn from Dixie that "de 'tilligent culed population on dis crek, days 'pointed me de litary cracker to sen 'butions to yer valable jernel," and it is a shame that Dixie did not pursue so promising a second career.

Other Blacks in the Cariboo included relatives of Mifflin Gibbs; his mother, Maria, lived in Barkerville for a time, along with another of her sons, I.P. Gibbs, and his wife. Little is known of this period in the family's history. Presumably they came west after Mifflin Gibbs's success in Victoria, but he himself says nothing about it in his autobiography. Like most other residents of Barkerville, the Gibbses suffered in the disastrous fire which destroyed the town in September 1868. John Anderson, the local correspondent for *The Elevator*, remarked that several Blacks had lost their homes and businesses: "Among the sufferers are our friends

W.D. Moses, I.P. Gibbs, and Miss Hickman. Mrs. R. Gibbs saved her things, but lost her house."

Whether Mrs. R. Gibbs was the wife of I.P. Gibbs is unclear, but she was certainly the Rebecca Gibbs whose poem on the great fire was published in the *Cariboo Sentinel* and later reprinted by *The Elevator:*

Come ye many sufferers and testify with me,
How this village flourished in the year of sixty-three;
Although it did lack nothing in the year of sixty-four,
It then sustained a thousand, aye a thousand men or more.

Still years roll on, until it reaches sixty-eight,
And we are still together, and with you I share my fate:
We hear distressed mothers and children in the street —
Inhabitants of Cariboo, why should we then not weep.

The Almighty architect, though wicked we have been,
Looked down and smiled upon us, when we commenced again;
We viewed this waste land village, with all her wealth and pride
As Sodom and Gomorrah — this cannot be denied....

The status of Black people in the Cariboo seems to have been one of general equality with whites. In clear contrast to the Victoria papers, the *Cariboo Sentinel* almost never criticized Blacks; the closest it came to racist stereotyping was a single mild "darky story," published in 1869. Blacks and whites shared accommodations, invested in mines together, and got drunk together. The miners' tolerance did not extend to the Chinese, who suffered considerably from white antipathy, but Blacks were usually seen as partners and allies. This attitude was most dramatically shown in the case of the Aurora Mining Company dispute, when Judge Begbie — out of personal bigotry or sheer pigheadedness — ruled against a company made up of Blacks and whites.

The case was a complex one, but the chief issue was whether the Davis Company (made up of Blacks and whites) had a claim to some land on Williams Creek which had been left unstaked by the white-owned Aurora Company. When the Davis Company struck gold on the claim, Aurora went to Judge Cox to assert their prior claim. Cox ruled in favor of Davis. Aurora ignored his ruling and dug a shaft on the claim; now Davis appealed to Cox, and again were upheld. The owners of the Aurora Company thereupon took the case to Matthew Baillie Begbie.

At the end of May 1866, Begbie agreed with Aurora's request for an injunction against the Davis Company that compelled the miners to stop working the disputed claim. Since he was elsewhere in the Cariboo at the time, Begbie ordered Cox to issue the injunction in his capacity as "Deputy Registrar of the Supreme Court." Cox refused, saying he held no such post and adding that he would resign it if he did.

In mid-June the case came to trial in Richfield. W.A. Farron, one of the white partners in Davis, told the jury that he had bought his shares in the company in June 1865, with no idea that the claim was disputed; he had even heard a shareholder in Aurora say that "nobody but niggers would look for gold there." The jury held that both companies' claims were weak, and recommended that "the said ground be equally divided, giving one-half to each." Unimpressed by this decision, Begbie offered to act personally as arbitrator; both companies agreed.

The judge took little time to reach a decision that startled everyone. Claiming that there was no evidence that Aurora had failed to stake the claim by the deadline, he observed: "The stakes are still standing there. I went on the ground myself and saw them a few days before the case came on in order to satisfy myself. I have not the slightest doubt that the stakes were put in by the 8th August." What would have been merely fatuous in a lesser man was magnificent stupidity in Judge Begbie; aware of the frailty of his own argument, he demolished it himself by adding that whether or not the land had been staked, everyone knew it belonged to Aurora and that Davis had had no right to claim it.

Having warmed to his task, Begbie now ruled that the land would indeed be divided between the two companies. He based his division on the fact that in August 1864, the Davis Company had been all Black, and on the theory that the Blacks had knowingly "jumped" the claim. The whites who had later bought out some of the Blacks had not known of the jump, and therefore received roughly one third of the disputed claim. Aurora got the rest; the Black miners got nothing.

After establishing this landmark of British Columbia jurisprudence, Judge Begbie went on his way. But several hundred miners gathered at the Richfield Court House two days later, in the first public meeting ever held in the Cariboo, to protest the decision. They were furious at the unfairness of the ruling, and alarmed at its implications: they now held their claims not according to law but according to the whim of Matthew Baillie Begbie. The miners passed three resolutions to make their views known:

"Resolved — That in the opinion of this meeting the administration of the Mining Laws by Mr. Justice Begbie in the Supreme Court is partial, dictatorial, and arbitrary, in setting aside the verdict of juries, and calculated to create a feeling of distrust in those who have to seek redress through a Court of Justice.

"That this meeting pledges itself to support the Government in carrying out the Laws in their integrity and begs for an impartial administration of justice. To this end we desire the establishment of a Court of Appeal, or the immediate removal of Mr. Justice Begbie, whose acts in setting aside the Law have destroyed confidence and are driving labor, capital and enterprise out of the country.

"That a Committee of two persons be appointed to wait upon His Excellency the Administrator of the Government with the foregoing resolutions, and earnestly impress upon him the immediate necessity of carrying out the wishes of the people."

Before the meeting ended, one of the white partners in the Davis Company was asked to speak. He was Frank Laumeister, a miner already famous for his attempt to introduce camels as pack animals in the Cariboo. Laumeister was understandably angry: "Mr. Chairman and Gentlemen," he told the miners, "I have actually nothing to say. I am one of the victims and stand victimized. Judge Begbie granted us a jury to try our case, that jury was sworn in and rendered their verdict and I was satisfied they had done what was right. Judge Begbie, however, came out two days afterwards with a sort of a revelation, he sent the jury's verdict overboard and instead of giving us half the ground...he gives us just about a quarter. We were advised by our counsel, who is an honorable gentlemen, that the Judge would decide as a friend between the parties, and he certainly gave us a sample of his friendship. He threw out our colored partners from any participation what-

ever in the ground, but these 'darkies' shall not suffer any loss by
me. If there is only a dollar comes out they shall have their pro-
rata share."

Laumeister and another miner were then chosen to take the
meeting's resolutions to New Westminster. When they presented
them to Arthur Birch, the administrator of the government, he
gave them little encouragement: Begbie would certainly not be
removed, but an appeals court might be set up after Vancouver
Island and British Columbia were united as a single colony.

The Black partners in the Davis Company were understandably
bitter, and one of them protested in the *Sentinel:*

"Sir, — Permit me to ask the following questions through your
valuable paper.

"First — Have we as colored men the right to pre-empt ground
for mining purposes?

"Second — Have we any rights in common with white men?

"Third — Why were our interests taken from us and given to
white men?

"I bought my interest in the Davis co'y and expended $2,900
before I received one cent out of said claim, and the dividends I
have received...have been appropriated to pay my debts in this
colony, but just at the time I was about to be rewarded, I have
been deprived of that portion of the Davis claim which would pay.
I have taken some pains to spread abroad the equality we as colored
men had, in the laws in an English colony, and am proud to say I
have found no difference until now.

"Poor Marshall lost his life coming to the Cariboo to look after
his small interest in the Davis co'y, the only pittance he had left
after 6 years hard work in this colony, and the only means of support for his family. His wife and four children are more in need of
the money than those to whom it was given. There are about fifty
colored men in and about Cariboo, the greater portion of whom
are miners, and the quicker we know our position in this colony
the better for us. Respectfully yours, COLORED MINER."

The editor's reply was sympathetic and understanding; however, as he pointed out, nothing could be done to overturn the
judge's decision. A day or two later, another white wrote to the
Sentinel to support the Blacks' cause, endorsing Laumeister while
reproving him for his use of the word "darkies."

It seems likely, from what we know of Begbie's character, that his ruling had been at least partly motivated by anti-Black bias. It is certain that popular outcry against him left him unmoved. Once, from a second-story hotel room, he had overheard men in the street plotting to kill him; his response had been to pour the contents of his chamberpot over them. A letter or two in the *Sentinel* would have been beneath the judge's notice.

Unfair though it was, the Aurora decision seems to have been an isolated incident, magnified by Begbie's status and power. In general, the Black miners appear to have enjoyed equal treatment in the boom towns of the Cariboo. Friendliness between the races there was probably due less to white tolerance than to the fewness of the Blacks and their disinclination to act as a political bloc in the way that Victoria Blacks did. In 1867, they even celebrated Emancipation Day in two groups—one of them pro-Union, the other pro-Confederacy. The whites detested the Chinese and distrusted the Indians, but those groups were alien and numerous whereas the Blacks were familiar and few.

Blacks were involved in a lesser gold rush in 1864, within a few miles of Victoria. An exploration team was making a preliminary survey of Vancouver Island's natural resources; near Sooke, about twenty miles west of Victoria, a group under Peter John Leech found gold in a small stream. The news failed to spark an immediate rush, but four Black men—Samuel Booth, George Munro, John Tyril, and William Dyer—formed a company and began serious prospecting on the newly named Leech River. They were almost immediately rewarded: Booth found a nugget as big as a hen's egg. The prospectors staked their claims, after which Booth and Munro took the steamer from Sooke to Victoria. The nugget was displayed for several days at the Wells, Fargo office; within a few days, many empty houses and stores showed signs explaining, "Gone to Sooke."

For a year or two, Leech River produced a reasonable amount of gold, and several prominent Blacks established themselves there. Willis Bond, orator and house-mover, returned to mining for a while, and Mifflin Gibbs made at least one visit. Richard H. Johnson, formerly an officer in the African Rifles, built the Mount

Ararat Hotel near the Leech River in the winter of 1864-65. Its good food and well appointed rooms were praised by Governor Kennedy, Douglas's successor, and the hotel did well for a time. But the diggings never compared with those of the mainland, and by the early 1870s the area had been abandoned by almost everyone but two Black prospectors and a few Chinese.

More slowly, but just as predictably, the fabulous wealth of the Cariboo also dwindled. From a crowded boom town, Barkerville shrank to a backwater; other settlements were deserted altogether. The gold seekers, Black and white alike, drifted on; only a few remained to ranch, cut timber, or mine coal. Of this population, a few were Black: Wellington Moses, for one, lived out the rest of his long life in Barkerville. Most of the Black miners made enough money to launch new ventures — or made nothing. Some of these men took up farming, and on Saltspring Island, forty miles north of Victoria, they helped to build a community that has survived to this day.

CHAPTER NINE

"They are the uncrowned kings."

The settlement of Saltspring Island was marked by many violent and dramatic events; Black people were involved in most of them. From our perspective, they seem epic figures, enduring hardships and giving immense, patient love and work to their land. The Black pioneers' lives and achievements have been well documented, but some modern writers have chosen to embellish their story, and it is sometimes difficult to distinguish fact from fantasy in the popular histories of Saltspring's early days.

Confusion even exists about the date and manner of the first Blacks' arrival on the island. Bea Hamilton, in her book on Saltspring, says that nine men landed together in the summer of 1857 to found a Black colony on the uninhabited island—but there were virtually no Blacks in the British Northwest until 1858 and there was never a Black "colony" on Saltspring. Sometime in 1858 or 1859, a group of Blacks reportedly asked Governor Douglas for permission to found such a colony, but were refused. Douglas may have been thinking of the fate of several Black communities in Canada: intended to help escaped slaves build new lives, almost all of these communities failed. It would be more sensible, Douglas felt, to promote a multi-racial settlement on Saltspring.

Saltspring's development was inevitable. By the late summer of 1858, many miners were already back in Victoria from the Fraser diggings. Too poor to resume mining or to return to their distant homes, they would somehow have to support themselves on or near Vancouver Island. A Scots-born lawyer, John Copland, had spent some years in Australia and was now especially concerned about the plight of other Australians; many of them were capable farmers, but could not get land. Settlement was legal only on land which the Crown had bought from the Indians and surveyed, and which cost an absurdly high $5 per acre. Since Douglas was always short of money, he had not been able to buy and survey enough land to meet the new demand, much less to sell it at a reasonable price. Copland therefore pressured the government to permit "pre-emption" of unsurveyed land by settlers who would not have to pay for it until it was surveyed — by which time the settlers would be prosperous enough to afford to buy it.

Saltspring was Copland's favored area for settlement. It was uninhabited (though the local Cowichans paid it seasonal visits); the Crown therefore had clearer title to it than it would to Indian-occupied land. Saltspring was mountainous, but well watered and possessing many good farming areas. Its climate was moderate, and it was relatively close to the new farms of the Saanich peninsula, north of Victoria. The island was rich in game; clams and mussels grew thick along its shores, and fish could be literally raked out of the waters around it. Its disadvantages were less obvious: the Cowichans, living on nearby Vancouver Island and other adjoining islands, considered Saltspring part of their territory, and resented the intrusion of newcomers. Though geographically close to Victoria, Saltspring could be reached only by occasional steamers or by dangerous canoe trips. And the wild game was preyed upon by wolves, bears and cougars that would soon learn to attack domestic livestock.

Nevertheless, the government approved Copland's proposal, and on 26 July 1859 it authorized twenty-nine settlers to pre-empt land on "Tuan Island," as Saltspring was sometimes called. While several of these twenty-nine were Black men, only one — Armstead Buckner — was among the seventeen who the next day left Victoria to take up their claims. Buckner settled north of Ganges, near St. Mary Lake; he was followed by numerous others. Among these were Abraham Copeland and his son-in-law W.L. Harrison; William Robinson, a gentle and religious man; John Craven Jones; Fielding Spotts; William Isaacs; Levi Davis; Daniel Fredison, and Hiram Whims. Louis and Sylvia Stark arrived in 1860, and soon became prominent in the community.

The Blacks were only one among many racial and national groups. Americans, Englishmen, Germans, and Polynesians also pre-empted Saltspring land. While some of their farms clustered around Ganges and other hamlets, most were scattered; an unmarried settler could claim 100 acres and a married one 200, so cabins tended to be isolated. Since one's neighbors were whoever took up adjoining claims, it was impossible to form a geographically distinct community of a single race.

Many of the first white settlers abandoned their claims after one winter, but the Blacks did well enough to bring their families to the island. For a time, therefore, they increased more rapidly than did other groups. In 1861, Rev. Ebenezer Robson visited Ganges, the largest of Saltspring's few small settlements. He noted in his diary: "There are in the settlement 21 houses on the same number of claims. Four of the houses [are] inhabited by white people and the remainder by colored people. I preached in the house of a colored man in the evening to about 20 persons all colored except three and one of them is married to a colored man."

This was to be an only temporary predominance; as settlement continued, the Black pioneers were soon again outnumbered by whites. But there was very little prejudice or hostility shown them by their white neighbors. When Mrs. Lineker — wife of an Australian settler — refused to worship in the same room with Blacks, Reverend Robson found her attitude unusual: "Poor woman she says some people might do it but she has been brought up so that she cannot — was the daughter of a church of England clergyman."

This lack of racial hostility was no doubt grounded in the same circumstances as in the gold fields. Confronted with a rich but dangerous country, Blacks and whites could not afford to be bigoted; prejudice was a luxury of Victoria's comfortable bourgeoisie. When a neighbor's help meant the margin of survival, it scarcely mattered whether he were Black, white, Indian, Hawaiian, or Maori. Nor could racism develop easily in the island's later years, since interracial marriages (as Robson observed) were common practice. Charles Irby, a Black historian, has cited one case in which a white Englishman on Saltspring married an Indian woman; one of their daughters married a Black man, and one of the daughters of this marriage in turn married yet another white Englishman. In another case, Irby quotes a descendant of the

Saltspring pioneers as saying that in one Black family "all the boys married white girls, and all the girls married white boys."

Certainly life for the Blacks was difficult enough on Saltspring even without bigotry. But the hardships they had already suffered made them tough and resilient in the face of danger. The Estes and Stark families are the best documented of Saltspring's Black pioneers, but they seem typical in their background and in their unyielding determination to overcome every obstacle. It is worth examining that background in some detail in order to understand what they and their neighbors achieved.

Sylvia Estes was born in Clay County, Missouri, in 1839. Her parents were slaves; her father, Howard, had taken his family name from that of his owner, a Scotsman named Tom Estes. Hannah Estes and their three children — Agnes, Jackson, and Sylvia — were the property of a German baker named Charles Leopold. Leopold was not a stereotypical slaveholder; he respected the abolition movement, and once risked injury to prevent a race riot at an anti-slavery meeting. His wife, however, treated their slaves badly. She and Hannah Estes sometimes quarreled, and after one kitchen argument Leopold exasperatedly chastised them both. Whatever his personal reservations may have been about slavery, Leopold demanded work from his slaves. Sylvia's earliest memories were of helping her mother dry dishes, and of looking after the Leopolds' children.

To be a child in slavery was to live in fear. Sylvia rarely left the Leopold property, having been warned of men who kidnapped Black children to sell in the south. She was regularly bullied by Mrs. Leopold, and forced to tend her master's children when she herself was sick. Visits by her father were rare events. But her parents raised her with love and firmness, and she even learned to read (though it was illegal) by being with the Leopold children as they did their schoolwork.

In 1849, Howard Estes and his master's sons were sent to California with a herd of cattle. Tom Estes promised to give Howard his freedom for $1,000, and agreed to let him work in California to earn the money. But when Howard sent the money, his master reneged. Howard sent another $1,000, this time in care of Charles Leopold. After a court battle, Tom Estes was forced to send Howard his "free papers," while keeping most of the second thousand dollars. By the time Howard Estes returned to Missouri in 1851, Agnes had died of scarlet fever and Sylvia had nearly died also. After some haggling with Leopold, Estes bought his family's freedom, paying $1,000 each for his wife and son, and $900 for Sylvia. Since Leopold had been offered $1,500 for Sylvia alone, he showed that he had at least some feelings.

Together as a family for the first time, the Esteses settled down on 40 acres. They raised pigs and chickens, and did fairly well for a time, but like other Black farmers they began to be harassed by white nightriders. In the spring of 1851, Leopold decided to drive a herd of cattle to California and asked the Estes family to come along as paid help. They agreed. The difficult journey took six months; once in California, the Estes and Leopold families went separate ways. Sylvia's family settled some sixty miles from Sacramento in Placerville, where they grew fruit and vegetables and where Hannah Estes took in the miners' washing. They prospered. Sylvia was to remember those years in California as the happiest of her life.

Sometime in the mid-1850s, Sylvia met and married Louis Stark, the son of a woman slave and her white owner. Stark had tried a number of careers before turning to dairy farming, and—like his father-in-law—he was doing well. But the worsening racial climate in California led both men to decide to emigrate to the British Northwest. Estes sold his farm and took his wife and Sylvia to San Francisco, where they embarked on the steamer *Brother Jonathan*. Louis Stark and Jackson Estes, meanwhile, drove fifty head of cattle north. The families were reunited in Steilacoom, Washington Territory, and went on together to Victoria. After several trips to outlying areas, Estes bought a farm in Saanich while Stark pre-empted land on the north end of Saltspring.

Sylvia by now had two small children, Emma and Willis, and was pregnant again when Louis brought her from her father's farm to their new home on the island. The day of their arrival was a violent and terrifying one for her.

The family reached Vesuvius Bay, on the northwest side of Saltspring, on a bright summer day in 1860. They had brought fifteen dairy cows, which were lowered into the water by ropes and left to swim ashore. The cows then plodded up the trail that led to the interior of the island. Meanwhile the Starks climbed down rope ladders from the deck of the steamer to two canoes. The paddlers, a local Cowichan and his wife, then took them ashore with their belongings. With them went a trader named McCauley; this man offered to stay with Sylvia and the children while Louis went up the trail to get help moving their goods to their cabin. The steamer left, and the little group was left alone on the beach.

As they waited, the Cowichans saw canoes enter the bay. There were at least seven of them, manned by Haidas. The Indian woman disappeared into the woods while her husband sat unmoving, evidently paralyzed by fear. The Haidas, natives of the Queen Charlotte Islands, were a fierce, far-roving nation who had often raided the southerners.

As the Haidas brought their canoes ashore, Sylvia could see that each canoe carried a cargo of furs. The northerners were en route to Victoria to trade. The Haidas examined the Starks' belongings with interest. One of them then turned to McCauley, waved a knife in his face, and asked in English: "Are you afraid?" Pale and trembling, the trader said he was not. The Haidas then offered to take the Starks' belongings up the trail. McCauley, who spoke their language, explained that Stark had already gone for help. Sylvia, meanwhile, sat on a log with her two children—Emma was about four, and Willis three—and prayed. "What will become of my children when they kill me?" she wondered. The Cowichan sat terrified nearby, not daring to look up.

When McCauley said he was going to Thomas Lineker's house at Ganges, the Haidas offered to take him. He accepted, and the canoes set out almost at once. But the Cowichan woman had taken her canoe across the narrow strait to Kuper Island, where there was a village of her people, and had told them of the Haidas' arrival. A war party set out at once, and overtook the Haidas as they were paddling down the eastern side of Saltspring toward Ganges. McCauley begged the northerners to put him ashore, but the Haidas decided to try to outrun their pursuers. They failed. The Cowichans surrounded their enemies, but after learning that McCauley was their passenger they allowed the Haidas to take him to Ganges. "We will not kill the white man," they called to the Haidas, "but we will kill you."

According to Sylvia Stark, the Haidas and Cowichans met in a. fierce battle on the bay after McCauley had been put ashore. If her account is accurate, McCauley must have been involved in two such battles that summer. On 9 July 1860, Thomas Lineker wrote to Governor Douglas to describe a massacre that had just taken place virtually on his doorstep.

"Sir

"At a meeting of the Settlers of this place I was deputed to address Your Excellency on the Subject of the Indians.

"I beg therefore to acquaint Your Excellency that on the 4th of July last, at noon, a canoe with nine men, two boys, and three women of the 'Bella Bella' tribe came in here with a person named McCauley who had business with some of the settlers. While he was talking with me, the Cowichians numbering some fifty, who were encamped here (& who on the arrival of the Bella Bellas manifested an unfriendly spirit, but afterward appeared friendly) commenced firing, a general fight Ensued which lasted about an hour, and ended in the Cowichians killing eight of the others, and carrying off the women and boys as prisoners, the fight occurred so close to my house, that I sent my wife and family into the woods for safety, during the night one of the Bella Bellas came to me, wounded. I pointed out a trail which would lead him to the Northern part of the Island, hoping he might get away. I felt I could not give him shelter without being compromised in this murderous affair. Two men have just arrived from the other side of the Island, who inform me that a week since some Northern Indians took two of another tribe out of their boat and cut their heads off.

"...Considering their defenceless position the Settlers trust that your Excellency will deem it expedient to afford them such protection as you in Your wisdom may think necessary."

Clearly, the Stark and Lineker narratives have enough in common to make one think that they deal with the same incident. It may be that only the canoe carrying McCauley actually entered Ganges harbor, where its crew encountered the Cowichans on land rather than on the water. Lineker's eyewitness account, written just after the massacre, is presumably more reliable than Sylvia Stark's description of a canoe battle she did not see. But we have no reason to doubt her own eyewitness account of the Haidas' arrival on the beach at Vesuvius Bay. Neither she nor Lineker was likely to confuse Haidas and Bella Bellas, and McCauley, as a trader, may well have traveled into Ganges with two separate groups in a brief space of time. Many northern Indians traveled to Victoria each summer, and no doubt there were many clashes between them and the local Indians; Lineker mentions the reported murder of two locals by northerners. We may never know the precise truth about the Indian battles of 1860, but it is certain that they did take place, and that Blacks and whites alike were frightened by the threat of involvement in Indian conflicts.

For the Starks, however, there were more immediate problems to contend with. When Sylvia and her children finally reached their new home, they found only a rough log cabin, still lacking a roof and a door. Neighbors helped Louis put the roof on, and a quilt was hung in the doorway. Still badly shaken by the incident on the beach, Sylvia was despondent and lonely. She later recalled three-year-old Willis trying to console her: "Don't cry, Ma. Let's go home." Home to him was California.

Nevertheless, the Starks persisted. Louis's first job was to clear his land, and he had little to do it with but some crude tools and his own ingenuity. To uproot stumps, he improvised an ox-drawn plough made from a V-shaped tree trunk. He also began a fruit orchard and planted some wheat. In addition to their cows, the Starks raised chickens, turkeys, and pigs; though the turkeys eventually went wild, and the pigs were preyed upon by bears, the family began to feel that it had gained a foothold.

Less than a year and a half after the Starks' arrival, Rev. Robson visited them and was impressed by their success: "...they with their children 3 in number are living on their own farm. It is good land and they only pay $1 per acre for it. Mr. Stark has about 30 head of cattle. He sowed one quart of wheat near his house last winter and reaped 180 qts. in the summer. One grain of wheat produced 2360 grains on 59 branches...His wife who was converted about 2 months ago filled my sacks with good things—4 lbs fine fresh butter, 2 qt bottles new milk. Mr. Stark gave me some of his large turnips." His liking for the Starks was reciprocated; Sylvia later recalled him as a pleasant and helpful house guest. Offered the Starks' best bed, he insisted on sleeping on the floor, and helped with chores—chopping wood, hauling water, and even churning some of Sylvia's "fine fresh butter."

Her conversion, in the late summer of 1861, had helped Sylvia to endure the loneliness and hardship of pioneer life. Her husband seems to have lacked her religious faith, and to have disliked the sight of his wife praying; she therefore went alone into the woods to pray. Robson noted in his diary that Stark was not as religious as he might have been, "and yet there are worse men than him in the church."

Robson urged the settlers to establish a school, and this was done by 1861; they built an unbarked log cabin in the Central Settlement which served as both schoolhouse and church. William Robinson, one of the earliest Black settlers, taught Sunday school there; another Black, John Craven Jones, used the cabin three days a week for regular classes and then walked up to Begg's Settlement to teach another three days. He was to teach all the island children for almost ten years without pay.

Jones came from a remarkable family. His father, Allen Jones, had bought his freedom in North Carolina and had tried to establish a school for black children there. Local whites burned it down three times. Moving his family to Oberlin, Ohio, Allen Jones saw four sons graduate from the college there. Three of these came to the British Northwest in the gold rush; John Jones stayed on Saltspring, while his brothers William and Elias moved on to the mainland. Elias eventually returned to the U.S., but William spent the rest of his life as a dentist and mining investor in the Cariboo. John Jones was widely admired and respected, and though his teaching left him little time to look after his farm, his pupils' parents saw that he was looked after. Jones had an assistant, Frederick D. Lester, who may have been a relative of Mifflin Gibbs's partner Peter Lester.

Several traditional accounts claim that John Jones persuaded his fellow Blacks not to arm themselves or to retaliate against Indian depredations; he is thus credited with preventing the massacre that such retaliation would have provoked. It is a good story, but an unpersuasive one. First of all, every farmer needed a gun for hunting, and would have laughed at anyone asking him to get rid of it; in fact, lead shot and gunpowder were Saltspring's chief imports in the early 1860s. Secondly, the story is based on a legend that the Indians singled out Blacks for special harassment, and would have risen en masse to avenge any injury done them by a Black.

There is no doubt that Blacks were robbed, threatened, and

sniped at by Indians, but little evidence that this was the result of a widespread Indian hatred of Black people. The Cowichans were understandably resentful of all encroachments on their territory, and some of them considered any unguarded cabin a fair target. Many farmers — Black, white, and Polynesian — saw their crops vanish overnight, picked by Indians passing through. But it is also true that many Indians got along quite well with the settlers, and were free to pick berries and hunt on the farmers' land just as they had always done.

From contemporary accounts, especially Sylvia Stark's, it appears that a few individual Indians were responsible for most of the harassment of Saltspring's pioneers. On one occasion, five Indians came unannounced into the Starks' cabin and began to examine everything in it — even counting the blankets on the bed. One of them took Louis Stark's rifle from the mantel; knowing it was loaded, Stark tried to take it away from him. In the scuffle, the gun went off, putting a bullet through the roof. Evidently frightened, the Indians left.

One Indian named Willie was especially notorious. He once tried to snipe at Stark, who saw sunlight glint off the Indian's gunsight. Himself armed, Stark called out to the Indian by name. Willie knew Stark's reputation as an excellent shot, and realized that if he missed, Stark would not miss him. He put up his rifle. Willie was later a prime suspect in at least one murder of a Black settler, and in his old age boasted of having killed thirty people.

Such incidents were to become more frequent in the late 1860s. They may have been inspired by the Indians' alarm over the loss of their lands, and by envy of the settlers' increasing prosperity. But the key factor in the growing violence between Indians and settlers was a disaster that shattered British Columbia's Indian societies for generations.

The winter of 1861-62 was one of the worst in the history of the Northwest Coast; it was so cold that for weeks the Fraser was frozen far upstream from its mouth, and on Saltspring over a hundred cattle died for lack of feed. Then, in March of 1862, a man arrived in Victoria from San Francisco with an advanced case of smallpox. As usual, thousands of Indians were encamped around the town; many were doubtless in poor condition after months of bitter cold. The newspapers warned of the danger of an epidemic among the native population, but as usual the authorities did nothing. Then, when smallpox did appear in the Indian camps, the government panicked and ordered all Indians to go home.

There had been smallpox outbreaks on the coast before, but they were minor compared to this one. Within days, the disease had spread from Victoria to Alaska; almost no Indian settlement escaped. Wilson Duff, in *The Indian History of B.C.*, estimates that 20,000 people — one third of the coastal Indian population — died of smallpox between 1862 and 1865. It was, by a wide margin, the greatest single catastrophe British Columbia has ever suffered. But since those responsible for it were white, and those killed were Indians, the epidemic has been passed over in B.C. history.

As it ran its course, the epidemic left Indian social hierarchies in ruins, adding to the misery of the survivors. As high-status positions became vacant through the deaths of their occupants, aggressive and ambitious young men rose rapidly. Their societies had always been warlike, but the experience and good sense of their elites had provided a brake against excessive violence. That brake was now gone, and both natives and settlers paid a heavy price.

The Stark family, ironically, suffered from the epidemic by their efforts to avoid it. Louis Stark had himself and his family vaccinated as the smallpox spread. In his case, the vaccination — together with the effects of working in cold, wet weather — made him ill. For several days, he was so delirious that Sylvia could not even leave him with the children long enough to fetch Dr. Hogg, Saltspring's only physician. While Louis's arm swelled, Sylvia had to milk fourteen cows, look after the pigs and chickens, and do all her usual household chores. She tried but failed to reduce the grotesque swelling of her husband's arm.

At last, when Louis was again aware of his surroundings, Sylvia left Emma to look after her little brothers; she left strict orders that Willis, then five, was not to be allowed outside for fear of cougars. After a long walk to reach the doctor, she returned with him in Armstead Buckner's cart. Dr. Hogg wrapped the arm in cold clay, which reduced the swelling. Though the affected arm was thereafter smaller than the other, Louis Stark regained his strength.

In the spring of 1863, three murders alarmed the settlers. Two men named Brady and Henley were attacked by Indians as they slept on an island near Saltspring; Brady died of his wounds. Then a German named Marks and his young married daughter were killed on Saturna Island. HMS *Forward* was sent to search the Gulf Islands for the killers. An Indian told the ship's officers that the murderers were in Penelakut, a village on Kuper Island. The *Forward* anchored off the village and a message was sent ashore, demanding the surrender of the suspects. The only response was a rifle shot that killed a sailor. The gunboat then methodically shelled the village to ruins; the Starks, on their farm a few miles away across the water, could hear the bombardment. According to Sylvia, a shore party then searched the village, but found only a blind old woman; the rest of the inhabitants had vanished into the woods. The culprits in the Marks killings were eventually found, however, and hanged.

For some years, lawlessness on Saltspring was relatively minor: thefts, assaults, and occasional snipings. Then, in the spring of 1868, William Robinson told his Sunday-school class that he would meet them only one more time; he had asked his wife to come west to join him, but she had refused, so he would be returning to her. During that week, a man arrived at Robinson's cabin at Vesuvius Bay to deliver some goods. The windowless cabin was locked, and no one answered when the man knocked. Trying again on Saturday, the man pried out some of the clay packed between the logs of the cabin, and was able to peer inside. He saw a man's booted feet. The constable was sent for, and a log removed to permit entry. William Robinson was found dead inside, shot in the back while eating his dinner. His killer had fired from point-blank range, and had then stolen a shotgun and some clothes.

Not long after, another Black was killed; his name was Giles Curtis, and he was found one morning with a bullet wound in his temple and his throat slashed. The settlers were now enraged as well as frightened, since the authorities seemed so slow to take steps against these killings. The government offered a $250 reward for Curtis's killer, and sent HMS *Sparrowhawk* to seek information in the Indian villages nearby. But the search got nowhere until the summer of 1869, when a Chemainus Indian denounced a fellow-tribesman for the murder of Robinson. The suspect was promptly tried, found guilty, and executed, though the case against him was based only on the testimony of the Indian who had turned him in.

Not long after this, Louis Stark wrote to Joseph Trutch — now the colonial land agent — advising him that he had moved his family to Ganges; since the death of Curtis, Stark had been unable to hire anyone to work on his relatively isolated farm. He may even have considered moving off Saltspring. An 1869 list of settlers pre-empting land in the nearby Chemainus district on Vancouver Island includes a "Lewis" Stark, and Sylvia recalled Stark's working a claim on Vancouver Island with a Black man named Overton. But if he did pre-empt a claim there, he almost certainly did not live on it. Until 1875 the family lived on their new farm, Fruitvale; when the Starks then moved to the Cranberry District near Nanaimo, Willis stayed behind to look after their Saltspring property.

Political life on Saltspring was rarely as intense as in Victoria. When the overworked settlers did act politically, it was usually to demand something from a colonial government that cared very little about them; in fact, Sir James Douglas was slow to appoint a Justice of the Peace for the island because he thought none of the residents competent to fill such a post. In their first election for an assemblyman, the settlers voted for John Copland, but he lost to J.J. Southgate — perhaps through fraud. John Jones was reportedly suggested as a possible candidate for the House of Assembly, but never ran. There does not seem to have been an instance in which voters split along racial lines; in 1868, however, Black voters may well have been responsible for the nongovernmental election of Mifflin Gibbs as the island's representative to the Yale Convention, which helped frame the terms of British Columbia's entry into Confederation.

The first elected body on Saltspring was a three-man school board which included Abraham Copeland, a Black. The board asked repeatedly that John Jones's teaching be officially recognized, and that he be paid a salary. It was pointed out that Jones had a first-class teaching certificate, and that the settlers had "18 children between the ages of 5 and 16 who are destitute of any opportunity of attending day school." Since Jones was also being sniped at and occasionally beaten up as he made his rounds, the government's slowness to pay for his services was all the more unforgivable.

In 1869, after nearly a decade of unpaid work, Jones was finally appointed officially, and thereafter paid $500 a year.

John Jessop, British Columbia's first Superintendent of Education, visited Saltspring on a tour of inspection in 1872. He was critical of the time Jones spent "itinerating between the Middle and Northern settlements...none of the children are more than three miles from the School-house and the road is improving year by year." Parents aware of cougars, bears, and snipers might have been as critical of Jessop's naiveté.

The superintendent was not much impressed with what he saw on his one-day visit to the northern school. Only two girls and a boy, out of seven children in the area, were present. F. Henry Johnson, in his biography of Jessop, quotes from the Superintendent's report: "The boy was working in Latin Grammar, having become such a proficient in English Grammar and Geography that those studies were dropped a year ago and Latin substituted! So the teacher reported. An examination in those branches did not by any means establish the fact of former proficiency." Given the nature of such examinations ("What is the usage of *that* as a Relative Pronoun; what other parts of speech might it be?"), it seems likely that Jessop was judging Jones's pupils by standards of rote learning. A safer estimate of Jones's abilities can probably be gained from the fact that he was a well liked and respected teacher who stayed on the job despite endless hardships. Most B.C. communities saw rapid turnover in teachers—one settlement had fourteen in five years—who were often detested by children and parents alike.

By the early 1870s, Saltspring was populous enough to warrant some self-government, and Letters Patent for the Township of Saltspring Island were issued in 1873. Of the seven councillors elected, two were Black—Jones and Henry W. Robinson, who acted as council clerk. Within a year, however, some settlers were protesting the council's actions, which were seen as committing taxpayers to needless and expensive projects. Though the controversy was a bitter one, no one seems to have raised the race issue; the division was between individualistic pioneers who wanted to be left alone, and "boosters" trying to develop the community.

Perhaps the best evidence for Black success on Saltspring Island is the fact that the Blacks' history became relatively undramatic

after the first violent decade. Among whites, Indians, and Polynesians, the Blacks became just another group—and not always
a distinct one, thanks to intermarriage. Most of the Blacks were
eventually to leave, but not because of discrimination. As agriculture developed in the Fraser Valley and Okanagan, farming
on Saltspring became only marginally profitable. For economic
reasons, the children and grandchildren of the Black pioneers
moved to Victoria, Vancouver, or even the United States. But the
contribution of those pioneers, though sometimes misunderstood
or distorted, was a real one, and will not be forgotten. As Marie
Stark Wallace said of them, they were men and women "willing
to go into the wilderness with axe and gun only, at their own risk...
whose courage and constancy blazed the trail and laid the foun-
dations...they are the uncrowned kings of pioneer days."

CHAPTER TEN

"The war of complexional distinction is upon us."

"Rotten egged. —A Negro forced his way into the parquette of the Colonial Theatre last evening, and was pelted with rotten eggs by some men in the gallery. Several white people were also struck by the missiles. The affair was very disgusting and highly reprehensible."

Such was the unfocused indignation of the *Colonist* in July 1860, when it recorded the first anti-Black incident in Victoria's theaters. Like the church dispute, the issue was integrated seating; but in a town much fonder of entertainment than of churchgoing, more people were involved. The Blacks had encountered racism right from the start of their settlement, but in most cases they had had powerful allies in church and government. In the theater controversy, those allies had no stake in the outcome, and left Blacks and whites to battle it out. This was to be the first of a series of such disputes in which the Blacks steadily lost ground as a community, though as individuals they continued to prosper.

In a booming frontier town, the theater was a major source of entertainment, and many performers came up from San Francisco to play to large audiences. When the Colonial first opened, it permitted integrated seating, but whites soon objected; the management thereafter allowed Blacks to sit only in the gallery. Strangely enough, no one seemed to mind sitting next to Blacks in the gallery, but the sight of a Black man in the more expensive parquette seats evidently provoked whites who could not afford them.

For some time after the "rotten egging," no Blacks seem to have challenged the theater's policy. Then, late in October, a Black named James Stephens was refused a parquette ticket. He and a number of other Blacks decided to make an issue of it.

On Saturday, November 3, the theater was two-thirds full as the curtain was about to rise on the first of the evening's two plays. There had been rumors that the Blacks intended to force their way into the parquette. The management had reminded its staff to sell no parquette tickets to Blacks; the box-office clerk had made a point of checking the color of the hands reaching through his wicket. Charlie Chinoople, the Bengali steward of HMS *Topaze,* was the only nonwhite allowed to buy a parquette ticket. At 7:30, two Black men came to the parquette entrance, which opened onto an alley alongside the building. They were refused admittance.

What happed next is unclear. The *Colonist* ran a long account of the incident which was almost certainly inaccurate in many respects. It reported that the two Blacks forced their way past John Wolfe, the doorkeeper, and took seats. Some of the audience shouted at them to leave; one of the actors offered each Black a dollar, saying: "Here's your money; go out." Wolfe then said the Blacks had not paid for their tickets.; another white grabbed one of the Blacks by the collar. The Black struck him, and a brawl erupted as costumed actors leaped from the stage and whites in the audience surged forward to take part. At this point, according to the *Colonist,* "a large number of negroes, armed with clubs, entered, and commenced striking right and left with their weapons." Before the police arrived to restore order, the theater had nearly been set afire by combatants throwing camphene lamps at one another.

Seven men, five of them Blacks, were arrested. The other Blacks left the parquette, and some bought gallery tickets. During an intermission, a Black who ventured into the pit "was rotten-egged by some white blackguards near him." This was not the last of the evening's incidents: two constables grew suspicious of three Blacks moving around the theater. The Blacks left the theater, but a constable detected a revolver under the coat of one of the men. He had to chase his suspect down Government Street and into the old Fort yard, where he found the man unarmed. Returning with the man, the constable found a loaded Colt six-shooter near the gate of the yard.

The *Colonist* graphically described numerous bloodstained victories of the riot, and asserted that "At one time the alley way outside the parquette entrance was filled with colored men, and it is thought there could not have been less than 100 present." It is likely that both the bloodshed and the number of Blacks involved were exaggerated; nevertheless, the incident triggered tremendous excitement. When the preliminary hearing was held the following Monday, the courtroom was so crowded that the windows were broken. At the hearing, four Blacks and two whites were ordered to appear in court again on the following Wednesday.

On the morning of the hearing, the *Colonist* ran a long editorial titled "The Colored 'Invasion.'" The writer, perhaps Amor De Cosmos, did his best to increase tensions and to threaten the Blacks: "Yesterday information was conveyed to the Superintendent of Police that the negroes were arming and preparing for a descent upon the theatre next Saturday night; and that deputations were expected from Salt Spring Island, New Westminster, and the American side, for the purpose of carrying out that design. If this report be true, it will be one of the worst steps ever undertaken by any class of men. It will raise...a storm of indignation and hatred on the part of the whites against the colored race.... Respectable negroes...will suffer alike with the guilty; and very few white people will be found willing to brave public opinion by giving employment to a man of color."

Having made these dire warnings against a hypothetical threat, the *Colonist* went on to assert its impartiality: "With us, a rowdy is a rowdy—no matter what the color of his skin." But it offered the Blacks a doubtful alternative to rioting: "If they had been denied admittance to the theater, the law was before them to appeal to. If no remedy could be obtained by applying to that source, they should have settled down quietly, and by uniform good conduct and moderation, trusted to a gradual change in public opinion, whereby they might be enabled to visit any portion of a place of amusement they saw proper." Implicit in this suggestion was the conviction that colonial law was too weak to stand against American bias; it was, tactically, a mistake to say so on the day of a hearing dealing with just that issue.

Judge Pemberton, no friend of De Cosmos anyway, heard the case. The theater's staff and actors were the chief witnesses. L. F.

Beatty, acting manager, stated the management's reasons for forbidding Blacks from sitting in the parquette. John Wolfe gave his version of the Blacks' entry, and several other witnesses confirmed his outline of events. What was not commented upon was the fact that it had been widely known before the incident that the Blacks intended to test the Colonial's color bar that night. Some whites had come to the theater armed with eggs and onions in anticipation of the event.

Pemberton dismissed charges against the two whites and one of the four Blacks, ordering the remaining three to stand trial the following week. Again, the *Colonist* kept the atmosphere acrid with an editorial warning Blacks against "a repetition of the scenes of last Saturday night." It also mentioned "a number of strange colored men" seen in town, thus keeping its readers edgy.

When the trial of Stephen Anderson, Adolph Richards, and George Washington was held on Monday, November 12, the trend of the testimony was sharply different from that in the hearing. While the whites repeated their earlier stories, defense attorney D. Babington Ring was able to cast doubt on them; he also proved that Anderson, at least, had obtained a parquette ticket. One witness refuted the assertion that Anderson and Richards had stormed in swinging sticks: Anderson, he said, had used his fists only after Wolfe grabbed him by the collar. The Black mob in the alley became instead a crowd of Blacks, whites, and Indians, mostly onlookers. The theater manager was stated to have invited the whites in the gallery to put the Blacks out — and thereby to have triggered the brawl. One witness did see "two or three sticks in the hands of the colored persuasion," but that was about the extent of the Blacks' weaponry. Judge Pemberton concluded that the Blacks had intended to test the theater's seating policy, but not to cause a riot; premeditation could not be proven, and he therefore acquitted the three defendants.

The issue died down for several months. Theaters were disreputable places for sober, churchgoing citizens; for middle-class Blacks, they were especially disagreeable, since in the gallery they would have to mingle with the roughest classes — Black and white alike — in Victoria. In the fall of 1861, however, a hospital benefit was staged, and the event attracted some of the town's most prosperous Blacks. Mifflin Gibbs was there, accompanied by his wife

Maria, who was pregnant. The couple had seats in the dress circle, just in front of Gibbs's old partner, Nathan Pointer, who brought his small daughter along. There were rumors that day that any Blacks in the dress circle would be pelted with onions or flour; one storekeeper had even given his customers free onions to take to the theater. A man named McCrea promised fifty dollars to one of the performers, Felix Lesbonis, if he would publicly refuse to sing in front of Blacks. Lesbonis refused the bribe, saying he had promised to perform whether Blacks were present or not. Gibbs and Pointer were aware of what was going on, but were determined to attend.

As the concert was about to begin, Emil Sutro — one of the scheduled performers — refused to go on unless the Blacks moved out of the dress circle. They were asked to do so, and refused. Sutro then left, and the concert began. Near its end, a number of listeners stood in the aisle between the dress circle and the regular seats. One of them tossed a newspaper package of flour; it struck Pointer and sent a cloud of flour over the Gibbses as well. Furious, the two Black men leaped to their feet and turned to see several white men facing them. Pointer gestured to one of them, a man named Ryckman, and shouted: "That's the man!" Gibbs promptly struck Ryckman, while Pointer hit a naval officer standing nearby. A short, sharp melee broke out, ending with the arrival of the police and the filing of charges against all involved.

The incident was of course a sensation, especially since the U.S. Civil War had been going on for six months and most of the Americans in Victoria had chosen sides. The *Colonist* editorialized on September 27 that the Blacks had every right to their seats, but added that since most whites were "opposed to colored people sitting promiscuously in the house, riots attended by loss of life will be likely to occur." In the same edition, Emil Sutro published "A Card," explaining his role if the affair:

'My name having been mentioned in connection with the 'Theatre Fracas' I wish to state what happened between Mr. Maguire, the leader of the orchestra, and myself. When I reached the theatre I learned that several colored people were occupying prominent seats in the dress circle, which caused considerable dissatisfaction to many English and American residents, preventing numbers from entering.... Mr. Maguire, after an interview with the parties, informed me that they were stubborn and would not budge an inch, to use their own expression. I refused then to play and left the theatre for home.... In concluding I would remark that I do not believe in any amalgamation of white and colored people, nor that the latter should socially intermix with the former. No sensible person will object to the colored population being admitted to any public place of amusement; but let one part of the house, no matter which, be reserved for their particular use, —where people will never intrude upon their society. They form a distinct class, and enjoy their full rights as citizens; but let these 'gentlemen' —if *they claim to be gentlemen* —not force themselves upon white society, where they are not desired, and are furthermore offensive to a majority of the residents of Victoria."

Sutro's statement provoked a stinging response next day from an anonymous Englishwoman:

"Now as regards the forcing themselves upon the 'white society,' allow me to say that they are as a class superior to many who composed the audience on the very night in question. Take for instance the unprovoked assault on those unoffending individuals. They have never forced themselves on society of any kind, and they have as much right, in a British Colony, to be seen and heard, as persons who are fortunate enough to possess a white skin. To say 'They enjoy their full rights as citizens,' is a flat contradiction of himself, for he says 'they were requested to resign their seats,' (although paid for) in favor of some white society. Which they very sensibly declined. Had they given an inch an ell might have been taken. As regards their being offensive to a large majority of the residents of Victoria, a very plain proof that they are not so is seen in the state of our churches, where nearly one-half of the congregations are *colored*. And on the night already referred to, I believe not one *respectable* person took part in the assault, which was as offensive to Englishmen as unwarrantable in an English Colony where all classes are truly free, and not so in name only. It would be well if Mr. Sutro would remember that he himself belongs to a much persecuted race which in some countries is a proverb and a byword. Remembering this, his sympathies should have been with, not against the colored people.

"All foreigners living on British soil should conform to British laws and customs, and not take upon themselves to dictate, and if

they cannot endure the presence of a colored man or woman, let
them by all means stay at home; they have full permission to do so,
and not offend anyone's eyes and ears by the disgraceful scenes
alluded to."

The letter was signed "an offended Englishwoman."

Mifflin Gibbs also published a letter in the *Colonist,* attacking
the paper's stand as too weak. He was obviously still angry, and if
some of his charges were intemperate they were at least understandable:

"I have resided in this Colony for the space of three or four years,
but never before visited a place of public amusement; but being
interested in the success of the Hospital fund to the amount of
several hundred dollars for provisions furnished the institution for
the comfort and sustenance of Americans and others whom misfortune had overtaken; and further, knowing it was to be under
the patronage of distinguished officials and the best English society
of the Colony, I went with my family, with no feeling than that
I would be exempt from the barbarous and insulting behaviour
that has characterized such places on former occasions — and for
that purpose purchased tickets for the dress circle. The public
knows the rest; how my friend — against whose respectability and
standing no exceptions can be taken — with his young daughter,
myself and wife were covered with flour, the performers pelted
with unsaleable fruit, and every effort made by the American rowdies to break up the entertainment.

"Now, sir, what course have you taken with regard to this outrage? You meet a colored man on the street and denounce it as
outrageous, the thing admits of no defence, the parties should
suffer for it, &c., &c. Often have you repeated that equal intelligence, equal standing, in a British colony secures equal treatment — shame, shame, &c. You hasten to your sanctum (as some
poor simple people thought) to indite 'words that breathe and
thoughts that burn' in vindication of outraged law. But lo! visions
of long advertisements and untold patronage from denizens of
Wharf street dance and glisten; the palms of your hands suddenly
expand and contract like a sunfish in greedy expectancy of the
thirty pieces of silver.

"You have little to say condemnatory, notwithstanding a great
wrong has been committed calling for condign punishment, you

admit the wrong, and in the next breath palliate the offence and invite repetition by carping about 'Caucasian and African,' 'deeply rooted prejudice,' 'social equality,' &c....

"That fact is patent that you, occupying the position of an Editor, and in the face of your continual clamoring for the faithful and impartial administration of British law as affecting other topics, have not only shirked your duty and proved yourself a trimmer...but have done worse. Instead of calling upon the authorities to have officers present to protect every man in the peaceful enjoyment of his rights, you wind up your article by advocating a course that would oppress and degrade a large and growing class of most loyal citizens. I have taken an oath of allegiance to Her Majesty's Government, paid the other day about $400 yearly taxes into the treasury; in return am I to be told by you that I shall be degraded on public occasions and proscribed to the Box, Parquette, or any other place, to please a few renegade Yankees, who, if they had a spark of patriotism about them, would be fighting their country's battles, and not be laying around here to save their hides and foment strife...."

The *Colonist* denied Gibbs's charges, somewhat patronizingly, and warned that "Mr. Gibbs is taking the right course to injure a just cause."

The assault cases stemming from the incident were brought before Judge Pemberton on September 30. The Blacks' lawyer tried to prove that the whites had attempted to influence at least one key witness, a Black waiter who worked in Sam Ringo's restaurant. While the waiter's story tended to implicate Ryckman, it was far from conclusive. Ringo himself—while denying that Ryckman had asked him to fire the waiter—also admitted he had lost some customers because it was known the waiter was going to testify.

Pointer and Gibbs asserted strongly that Ryckman had thrown the flour, but a number of other witnesses denied it; one of them, a carpenter of HMS *Topaze* named Robert Shaw, declined to say whether he himself had thrown the flour. Pemberton might have found Shaw in contempt of court for refusing to testify unless the carpenter was willing to say it was to prevent "self-crimination." Shaw would not do so, but Pemberton did not find him in contempt. The judge then acquitted the four whites charged in the incident. When the court turned its attention to the whites' coun-

tersuit, Gibbs admitted assaulting Ryckman and was fined five
pounds; the charge against Pointer was dropped for lack of evidence.

The theaters now made their policies public by stating on their
handbills and posters that Blacks could be seated only in the gallery. Bitterly angry, the Blacks petitioned Governor Douglas over
the issue, and reminded him of the promises he had made in 1858:

"Coming to this colony to found our homes, and rear our families, we did so advisedly, assured by those in authority that we
should meet with no disabilities political or conventional on the
ground of color." The middle-class nature of their protest was
clear; the petitioners condemned theater segregation in general,
"but the outrage is still more apparent, when it is known that the
gallery is the...resort of the lowest order." Evidently believing that
mere citizenship was inadequate grounds for equal treatment,
they even resorted to special pleading: "Your memorialists...com-
pare favorably with any other class; — they are in possession of
real estate to the amount of 50,000 pounds, which awaits taxation
for the support of the Government. We are here investing our
means, and zealously laboring for the well being of the colony...
and desire to have our families untrammelled by the perpetuation
of a mean and senseless prejudice against color — a prejudice having no foundation that is honorable, and alone supported by the
ignorance and brutality of the lowest order of society...We therefore petition your Excellency to make such recommendations that
will guarantee the rights of your petitioners in common with all
other men.

"Signed on behalf of Two hundred and Sixty colored residents
                         Wellington D. Moses
                         Jacob Francis
        Committee: F. Richard
                         Wm. Brown
                         Richard H. Johnson"

Douglas met with the committee when it presented the petition,
but was evidently unable or unwilling to act for the Blacks. The
issue seems to have died down for a couple of years; then, in
December of 1863, a Black man named Alexander McCarthy was
arrested after a disturbance when he insisted on taking a seat in
the dress circle, for which he had a ticket. In court next day, Mc-
Carthy's lawyer argued that since there was no law forbidding

Blacks from sitting anywhere in the theater, anyone — Black or white — had a right to the seat for which he had a ticket. This argument had some effect, for the judge dismissed the charge of creating a disturbance; however, he fined McCarthy for resisting the constable who had arrested him.

The incident provoked another test case involving a veteran of the 1860 theater riot, Adolph Richards, along with Fortune Richard and James Fountain. Having obtained tickets through a white friend, they went to the Colonial Theatre and were refused their seats. The Blacks then sued the manager for $500 each, but lost their cases.

By now the issue must have been a maddening one to Victoria's Black middle class. Many of them would probably never have dreamed of attending, since theaters continued to have a seamy reputation. But to be explicitly relegated to the lower-class seats was to be challenged on the very principle that had brought them to the colony.

To lose battle after battle did not discourage them, however. A visiting American Black attended the theater in the spring of 1864, and though the ticket seller tried to discourage him, he asked for and received box seats; there was no reaction from white patrons. The visitor evidently expected none, for he went accompanied by ladies, also Black. Others may have been encouraged by this quiet success, for later in the year the manager of the Victoria Theatre printed a handbill advising his patrons that "colored persons cannot be admitted into the Dress Circle or Orchestra Seats. Should they feel disposed to visit the Theatre, he will cheerfully fit up and comfortably furnish for them an eligible portion of the building; but he will not expose his audience to the disturbance and danger too likely to arise out of disputes about place, position, or precedence."

Once more a committee petitioned the governor — Arthur Kennedy, Douglas's successor. On the same day, the governor's colonial secretary replied: "While his Excellency regrets that he is unable to remove the invidious distinction thus drawn between classes of Her Majesty's subjects, he desires to assure you that he has no sympathy with those who would make creed or color a barrier to any of Her Majesty's subjects attaining and occupying any social position to which their character and capacity may entitle them."

This vacuous sympathy was all the official support the Blacks got. But time was on their side. In November 1865, John Dunlop was barred from the Victoria Theatre. He was probably the last Black to suffer this discrimination. With the gold rush over and the U.S. Civil War ended, Victoria had become a stagnant small town, and the theaters were hard pressed to fill their seats. Many Blacks had returned to the United States; so had many white Americans. There was less resentment shown to the Blacks who remained, and theater segregation ended forever. Mrs. Ruth Ford, whose mother was born in Victoria in 1872, recalls her mother's account of the Blacks in the audiences of the 1870s and '80s: "They were apparently diligent spectators, and galas at the Victoria Opera House were notable for the large groups occupying the best seats, and the beautiful gowns and jewels of the women. They certainly made a lasting impression on the girl who became my mother."

Another long-lived dispute concerned Victoria's saloons, many of which were owned by Americans who usually refused service to Blacks. The saloon-keepers were also active in politics, and in general supported De Cosmos and other reformers. After the election of January 1860, one Black publicly criticized two of De Cosmos's backers for refusing service to Black voters who had supported Cary and Franklin: "One of Cary's voters was ordered out of Carroll's Saloon on Yates Street, barely for looking in at a crowd of drinkers...Mr. Bayley has also asserted that not another colored man shall approach his saloon again; what a petty revenge...for my part I do not use the article he vends there."

J.D. Carroll would later nominate Jacob Francis in a race for an Assembly seat, but at this point he was very much against the Blacks. His bookkeeper, just after the 1860 election, entered another saloon and, without provocation, struck a Black man with a stick. De Cosmos played up the beating the bookkeeper then received, but ignored its cause. When a Black named William Bastion ordered a glass of ale in Carroll's saloon, he was charged fifty cents; Bastion took Carroll to court for extortion, but the case was dismissed.

A similar incident involved Jacob Francis a few months later, when a saloon-keeper refused to sell him two bottles of champagne. Francis sued for damages, but lost when the jury ruled that the saloon was legally an inn; since Francis had not been a guest at the inn, he was not entitled to service. Francis made another attempt to get equal treatment in 1862, when he went into the American-owned Bank Exchange Saloon with three white friends. The whites were served, but not Francis, who promptly took the saloon-keeper to court. Judge Pemberton held that no saloon license would be given to anyone who refused to serve Blacks; however, he also said that private bars could be set up on the premises, and that Blacks might be excluded from these.

Despite these frustrations, Victoria's Blacks continued to contribute to the community, and in August of 1862 Mifflin Gibbs ran for city councillor in the new municipal government of Victoria. His first speech was at an all-candidates' meeting; perhaps intentionally, the *Colonist* reviewed it rather than reporting what he said: "Mifflin W. Gibbs (colored) delivered a longwinded and flowery address, but many portions of it were well received, and although it had the effect to thin the house, taken all in all it was a very creditable effort." At least his name was correctly spelled; De Cosmos was fond of spelling it "Miften," and in a later story he was referred to as "W. Gibbs."

Gibbs himself was not very specific in print. On August 15, following the custom of the time, he placed an advertisement in the *Colonist* which was graceful but vague:

"Having been requested by many of my fellow-citizens of all classes to stand for the Office of City Councillor...I therefore offer myself for the same.

"Believing that men's actions are the best interpretations of their principles I have little to say of a promissory character, but would be happy to meet them at an early date, and speak of the necessities of the hour, and my course if you do me honour to return me."

Perhaps a few electors managed to discuss the issues personally with Gibbs, but it is unlikely; the election was held the next day. Thomas Harris—the butcher and sheriff who had freed Charles Mitchell from the *Eliza Anderson*—was elected Victoria's first mayor by acclamation. The six hundred voters then turned to the election of councillors. Since each vote was public, there was genuine suspense in the outcome. The *Colonist* found Gibbs's bid the most interesting, and described the course of the voting in some detail:

"Much speculation as to the probable result was rife until half past one o'clock, when a number of colored voters having been polled (some of them plumpers) it became obvious that the colored candidate (Gibbs) would come very near an election if he did not succeed in gaining a seat—it being known that the colored vote numbered about thirty-five, and it becoming also known that some fifty white electors had pledged themselves to him. At half past one o'clock, Gibbs stood on the list with Messrs. Copland, Reid, Hicks and Stronach alone leading him; but in a few minutes several votes for Searby were recorded, changing the complexion of the poll and placing Gibbs sixth with Lewis five votes behind. It then became evident...that the fight was between Lewis and Gibbs as to who should stand sixth on the list of successful candidates—and from the hour of two o'clock until the close of the poll at four, the friends of each party worked like Trojans for their respective favorite.... Lewis slowly gained on Gibbs, and by half past three o'clock, was eight votes ahead of him. Some twenty votes were cast after proved in this case—it was difficult to determine, amid the buzz and confusion, which of the two—Lewis or Gibbs—would prove to have been successful."

In fact, Gibbs lost to Lewis by just four votes, 98 to 94; the next closest candidate polled only 70. Gibbs seemed to feel there had been some irregularities in the election, for on August 20, just as Chief Justice Cameron was about to swear in the new council, Gibbs handed him a written protest against Stronach's right to sit as a councillor. Cameron refused to accept the protest, saying it would have to be in the form of a petition. Without argument, Gibbs withdrew his protest and the ceremony proceeded.

For Gibbs, however, the municipal election of 1862 was only a temporary setback, and it seemed to demonstrate that the Black community was now a genuine political power in the colony. In 1863, a new House of Assembly was to be elected; this time there were 52 Black voters whose qualifications were unquestionable. De Cosmos was running again, and did not intend to be thwarted for a third time. He therefore turned to the Blacks for support. According to a report in the rival *Daily Chronicle,* De Cosmos spent two hours with Gibbs, trying but failing to win his vote. When the Blacks held a public meeting to discuss the election, De Cosmos attended, but he must not have enjoyed what he heard. A white quoted De Cosmos as promising to "drive the damned niggers from the colony." Willis Bond accused the editor of causing untold misery to many Blacks in the colony; Gibbs said that De Cosmos should be "put on his good behavior for three years before the colored people would vote for him." Speaking directly to De Cosmos, he said: "If you are elected we will see if your professions are sincere; if you are defeated we will see how you behave yourself under the disappointment."

But Gibbs and his associates must have been aware that the Black vote was far from united. On election day, 18 July 1863, an advertisement appeared in the *Daily Chronicle:* "The colored voters will poll FIFTY-TWO VOTES. Whichever way their influence is cast today, so goes the election! The colored man who falters in the present emergency and votes for his arch-enemy will betray his race."

The appeal failed. Some of the Blacks neglected to vote; some even voted for De Cosmos, who was elected. James Pilton speculates that "Perhaps some preferred to make a friend of the enemy. Since there was no secret ballot he would know how each had voted by merely consulting the poll books. Perhaps there were social or economic reasons why a few Negroes gave him their vote. Did some realize the hostility aroused against them by bloc voting?" These may all have been factors, but a more likely one was the fact that the Blacks were individuals — and individualists. The immigrants of 1858 had resolved not to segregate themselves; the voters of 1863 showed that they still held to that resolution.

Even sharper divisions appeared in the Black community in January 1864, when a by-election was called to fill a vacant seat in the Assembly. Despite their split vote the year before, the Blacks were still a group worth courting, and W.M. Searby, a city councillor, set out to win them over. For Gibbs and other American-born Blacks, the chief issue in this election was a colonial law allowing only British-born subjects to hold seats in the Assembly; naturalized subjects were denied this right. The law seemed clearly aimed at keeping Blacks out of the Assembly, since most of the settlers naturalized under the Alien Act of 1861 were Black men.

A bill to remedy this injustice had been proposed at the last session of the Assembly. It would give naturalized subjects the same rights as the British-born after a five-year residence in the colony and the swearing of an oath of allegiance. Gibbs and Searby exchanged letters on this subject, which were published in the *Colonist;* Searby promised "to vote for such a measure whenever it is introduced into the House of Assembly should I be elected."

To many Victoria voters, this promise must have seemed as cynical and expedient as Cary's use of the Blacks to steal the election of 1860. Searby had been a strong ally of Reverend Macfie during the church dispute, and in 1862 he had said publicly that he would refuse to sit on the city council if any Black man were elected to it. In addition, Searby's chief opponent was Selim Franklin, who had been the chief beneficiary of the Black vote in 1860; now, however, he had lost their support by refusing to endorse the proposed bill.

Franklin's candidacy was strongly backed by the *Evening Express,* which bitterly attacked the Blacks. One editorial warned that the "Alien Bill" would enable Gibbs and his partner Peter Lester to enter the Assembly; it went on to assert that all other aliens in the colony wished neither to give up their citizenship nor to meddle in their hosts' politics. Only the Blacks — citizens, the writer claimed, of no country — wanted to enter the Assembly.

Another editorial was particularly patronizing in its advice to Black voters: "We believe that on calm reflection their modesty will reassert its sway over their minds, and that, when this little temporary ebullition of ambitious yearnings has passed away, that they will be ready to acknowledge their own interests, and also the interests of the community, are best served by leaving the legislation of the Colony in the hands of their English friends."

Given such attitudes in the white community, one might have expected the Blacks to close ranks behind even so doubtful an ally as Searby. However, the Jamaican Blacks felt no need to support him or the Alien Bill. British-born, they saw no benefit to themselves in the bill, and Searby's record made him all the more unattractive. J. Cathcart, one of the Jamaicans, sent a long and angry letter to the *Evening Express:* "My friends among the Aliens," he wrote, "...don't mistake a political and electioneering dodge for a philanthropic measure." Predicting that Searby would break his promises if elected, Cathcart went on to say: "I am doggedly arrayed against any foreigners assuming the reins of government." Nationalism, then, was stronger than racial ties. To Cathcart, the American-born Blacks were still foreigners.

There was a heavy vote, and virtually every qualified Black cast his ballot. For a while, it looked as if the American-born Blacks would elect Searby, but the final count gave him only 174 to Selim Franklin's 181. Only three American-born Blacks had voted for Franklin, but all the Jamaicans had, and they gave him the margin of victory.

Furious and frustrated, a number of Blacks met in Ringo's saloon after the election and passed resolutions condemning the "certain class of colored men, calling themselves Jamaicans," who had betrayed the cause. They also called for a boycott of Jamaican businesses, especially Cathcart's. Peter Lester and Willis Bond were the leaders of this meeting; Gibbs, more prudent, stayed away. For one part of the Black community to turn on another could only harm everyone, and Gibbs must certainly have remembered De Cosmos's appeal for a boycott of Black businesses after the 1860 election.

Nevertheless, the anti-Jamaican resolutions were sent to the *Pacific Appeal,* a Black newspaper in San Francisco, and the incident helped to divide the Blacks along national lines. Whether they liked it or not, the American-born Blacks were treated as Americans; and even as their political influence weakened, they felt compelled to try to enforce an uncomfortable and impractical unanimity on themselves.

As the Civil War went on, the Blacks found themselves almost powerless to combat the growing racism in the colony. The Victoria Pioneer Rifle Corps (the African Rifles) were among the first to suffer from it. In 1862, the Black militia unit asked the government for financial help; Douglas did not even bother to reply. A year later another appeal failed, and the colony officially stated that it had no militia at all. This official neglect had several causes. Douglas was as reluctant as ever to spend money, least of all on a politically controversial group. Anti-Black feeling was intense in the colony by this time, and the government saw no reason to provoke either faction of Americans in Victoria. There seemed little need for a militia in any case, since the threat of an Anglo-American war had faded. (Local Confederate sympathizers, however, at one point plotted to fit out a privateer which, using Victoria as a base, would prey on Union shipping off San Francisco and perhaps embroil Britain in an incident. Like similar schemes in Ontario, Quebec, and the Maritimes, this one got nowhere.)

The African Rifles persisted. In January of 1863 eight of the militiamen formed the Victoria City Brass Band. The unit's ban against whites was relaxed to allow the bandmaster of HMS *Topaze* to train the new musicians. In May, the unit held an evening of entertainment in its drill hall to raise money. The women of the Black community, already experienced in raising funds to help freed slaves in the Union States, were a major source of assistance as well. But not enough was raised, and when yet another appeal to Douglas was turned down, the corps became inactive for the rest of the year.

Early in 1864, the African Rifles revived as plans were made to welcome Douglas's successor, Arthur E. Kennedy. The committee responsible for the welcoming ceremonies was approached with the suggestion that the corps march in the parade. The committee agreed, on condition that the militiamen's uniforms and equipment were adequate. The news caused a stir in Victoria, prompting many sarcastic letters in the newspapers; one suggested that the Blacks' appearance in the parade would at least amuse the new governor. No one made color the issue, however; critics attacked only the unit's supposed inadequacy.

Early in March, officers of the Victoria Pioneer Rifle Corps asked the Colonial Secretary for rifles with which to drill in preparation for the parade, and pointed out that they were paying a drill sergeant five dollars a day to train them. The rifles were promptly delivered, and the VPRC went on with its preparations. It was sustained by the renewed interest of the Black community and spurred by continuing attacks from whites. An absurd rumor was circulated that the Blacks were prepared to force themselves, with loaded rifles, into the parade if they were refused an official place in it. It was also charged, perhaps accurately, that the whole controversy was really a political skirmish between white factions: Douglas's men had kept Blacks from attending the old governor's farewell banquet, but were trying to get the African Rifles into the welcoming parade as a way of embarrassing Kennedy's supporters.

At length the committee in charge of the parade decided to reject the Blacks. Predictably, it claimed to do so not because of its members' prejudice but rather because of others'. A military unit by custom would march at the head of the parade, and the committee feared that the other marchers—especially the volunteer fire brigades—would refuse to take part. However, the committee failed to advise the VPRC officially; the unit therefore announced that it would report to the Marshal of the Day like any other group in the parade. At this the committee officially advised the VPRC that it would not be marching. The Blacks nevertheless continued to drill, and marched through the streets in the evenings. On March 14, they held a special ceremony, open to the public, at which the women of the Black community presented the unit with a silk Union Jack. As reported next day in the *Daily Chronicle,* the presentation was made by Sarah Pointer, wife of Gibbs's ex-partner. After laying the flag across the drum, Mrs. Pointer read an address to the corps:

"Captain and members of the Victoria Pioneer Rifle Company: In behalf of the ladies of Victoria, I present to you this flag. It affords us much pleasure to do so, as we know your loyalty to this government is proverbial. The fostering care it has shown to the oppressed of our race leaves us under many obligations to the sagacity and wisdom of her statesmen. Yet in this far distant Colony of Her Majesty's dominion we have many causes to complain. True, you have not as yet been called on to rally under this flag for its protection; yet the war of complexional distinction is upon us, and is more ravaging to us as a people than that of Mars.

"But men, as long as this flag shall wave over you, you may rest assured that no man, or set of men, or nations, can successfully grind you down under the iron heel of oppression. Then, soldiers, look up to this insignia of liberty, that has waved a thousand years over the battle and the breeze. In committing this color to your charge, we only hope that you will guard it well, and yourselves be as untarnished as the color. It will inspire you in the hour of peril; it is a nation's proudest boast; 'it's a terror to a foe, and a canopy of peace to a freeman.'"

On March 25, Kennedy arrived and was greeted by a huge parade. The African Rifles, however, marched to a Black-owned restaurant near Beacon Hill, where they ate chicken and drank beer. A week later the unit paraded to the legislative buildings to deliver an address to the new governor. After congratulating Kennedy on his safe arrival, the address raised the issue of discrimination: "Our only regret is that...we were precluded on account of an anti-English prejudice against our color of doing ourselves the honor as well as pleasure of taking part in the procession as a military company...which with all its imperfections is at least the only representative of the British volunteer element in the Colony."

According to some sources, Kennedy is supposed to have responded ungraciously by urging the African Rifles to disband. In fact, the new governor was very cordial. He was aware of the colony's race problem, he told the Blacks, and would do all he could to "heal the breach" between them and the whites. Kennedy dissociated himself from prejudiced whites, saying that in the first colony he had been sent to, the Gold Coast, the Chief Justice and clergy had been Blacks. Then, rather smoothly, he urged his listeners to be patient and forbearing, and to await the eventual dissipation of prejudice. Having heard such advice before, the Blacks were probably unsurprised to find Kennedy as reluctant as Douglas to give them any official backing. They held their fourth annual election of officers in April 1864, but meetings and drills became far less frequent.

In the spring of 1865, the *Colonist* — which had praised the VPRC on several occasions — wondered: "What has become of the Pioneer Rifle Company, which at one time promised to become a very efficient and soldier-like body? Surely the enthusiasm and military ardor of our colored citizens has not evaporated? The brave and warlike deeds of their countrymen in the ranks of the Federal armies should incite them to emulate so far as circumstances will permit, the patriotism of their American brethren." (Presumably the word "countrymen" meant fellow-Blacks, since most if not all of the Black militiamen were British subjects.)

Richard H. Johnson, a former captain of the VPRC, wrote a reply next day; speaking of the volunteer's morale, he said: "Allow me to inform you, Mr. Editor, with all respect, that their enthusiasm and ardor as far as this colony is concerned have evaporated. The mean and scandalous manner in which they were treated upon the advent of Governor Kennedy is still fresh in their minds. Having as much human nature under their dark skins as others of a paler hue, they cannot readily forget the snubbing they received on that occasion. Although being the first...military organization on the Island, after having gone to great expense in purchasing land, building a hall, paying a drill master, and supplying themselves with uniforms, and although having taken the oath of allegiance to her Majesty, they were by a direct vote of a Committee (composed of British subjects) for His Excellency's Reception, prohibited from forming part of the procession to receive him. Nor is this all — there has ever been a studied effort to ignore their existence, to dampen that 'ardor' and chill that 'enthusiasm' for which you enquire. The Volunteer Rifles [a white unit] though last in the field and well able financially to sustain themselves, have had a handsome sum voted for them by the House of Assembly, the barracks given them for drill purposes, with every other stimulant necessary to foster efficiency. In a word, Mr. Editor, the authorities seemed ashamed of us, and we were disgusted with them."

A year later, the Colonial Secretary belatedly asked for the return of the rifles loaned to the unit for the parade two years before. They were returned at once, along with a letter stating that the VPRC had not disbanded, but had not met for drill because of government discouragement and the depletion of its ranks by Blacks returning to the United States.

Other incidents had by then deeply discouraged many Black colonists. In 1864, Peter Lester and Mifflin Gibbs had been refused tickets to the banquet honoring Governor Douglas on the eve of his retirement. Douglas did nothing to correct this injustice to his longtime supporters. A few weeks later, Blacks were barred from a public-subscription banquet to celebrate the Queen's birthday; the remarkable reason given for this was that the colony's American residents were opposed to Black attendance. As James Pilton observes, "Why the Americans should have the right to prevent British subjects from attending a British banquet celebrating the birthday of a British queen, defies an answer."

Clearly, anti-Black bias had become widespread in Victoria. A temperance society and a literary group had been disbanded after Blacks had joined them. Black and white Masonic groups never met together, and white women never socialized with Black women outside church. The Americans' anti-Black attitudes, real or imagined, served as an excuse for growing numbers of biased English residents.

American Blacks were well aware of Victoria's racial tensions. In the spring of 1864, an anonymous correspondent for the *Pacific Appeal* visited the city, and his account was soon reprinted in *The Liberator,* William Lloyd Garrison's widely read abolitionist weekly. The article summarized the status of the Blacks in perhaps their worst year, and may have overstated their difficulties.

"There is as much prejudice," the correspondent wrote, "and nearly as much isolation, in Victoria as in San Francisco. In some cases, the social and political position of the colored people is more favorable there than here; but the Americans and Jews from California, who have settled here, have formed a public opinion unfavorable to us. Happily, they have not been successful in all cases. Churches and schools are exceptions, although our leading men had to fight hard to obtain their rights in both. Messrs. Lester, Gibbs, J. Francis and others, battled manfully to keep churches and schools free from caste; and to their exertions is due the equality which exists in those institutions. It was grudgingly and unwillingly awarded; but they claimed it as their right as British subjects, and finally succeeded.

"I went to the theater with some ladies.... When I said I wanted box tickets, the man hesitated, and said he believed the boxes were full; but as I insisted, he gave me them, and we found very eligible seats.

"Colored men are never summoned as jurors on trials; I believe they have occasionally sat on coroners' juries. When they were organizing fire companies, Jacob Francis endeavored to have the colored inhabitants represented, but he was voted down. In some places of public accommodation, such as barber-shops, bar-rooms, restaurants and hotels, colored persons are denied the usual privileges; but such places are invariably run by Americans or foreigners. In many of the finest establishments, where the proprietors are Englishmen, there is no distinction; they are free from the prejudices which Americans have introduced. There are, however, many Englishmen who are as full of prejudice as the lowest secesh [secessionist] American among them. They all, moreover, receive you with an aristocratic, patronizing air.

"Among the notables of Victoria is the celebrated Archie Lee, upon whose fate once hung the destinies of the colored people of California. Archie is a sober, honest, hard-working man, a respectable citizen of Victoria, and a loyal subject of Her Majesty. It affords me much pleasure to be able to contradict the reports which have been circulated prejudicial to the character of Archie Lee; he follows the lucrative occupation of draying, and has accumulated some property, and is much respected by the community.

"The colored inhabitants of Vancouver Island are in advance of the colored people of San Francisco in point of wealth. They nearly all own real estate, and are in comfortable circumstances. They went to Victoria during the Frazer river excitement of 1858 — some to engage in mining, some to live under the fancied liberality of British laws, and some to engage in speculation.... As regards intelligence and acquirements, they present an average of the colored people of this and Eastern cities....

"I referred to the political position of the colored people. They have the elective franchise, and that is all the political privilege they do possess. The naturalized subjects are eligible to seats in the city council, but not in the provincial parliament, a law being passed to exclude from that body all except subjects of the British Empire by birth. This law was evidently passed to exclude colored persons, for since 1858 only 4 white persons have become naturalized; whereas, about 150 colored persons have taken the oath of allegiance. It is not very probable that a colored person will ever be elected to either body. Two attempts have been made; and although, in each case, the candidate was as capable and worthy as any in the colony, they were both defeated. Prejudice is too strong in Vancouver Island. We have brighter prospects of political elevation under our own Government, than in any British colony on this coast."

The correspondent's opinions were no doubt generally accurate, but he seems to have minimized the support Blacks received from many white Victorians. In the school and church disputes, the clergy had strongly backed the Blacks' right to integration. The visitor had relatively little trouble at the theater, evidently having expected none. It was true that Blacks had been barred from jury duty since 1860; this was a step backward, for when the first Black jurors had been named, the *British Columbian* (a paper published in New Westminster) had applauded the event as an example of British fairness. Not until 1872 would Blacks sit on juries in the province.

No doubt the racist atmosphere of Victoria in the early 1860s had many causes: the tensions of the U.S. Civil War, the visible prosperity of many Blacks, and the renewed rigidity of class barriers as American influence waned. One contemporary, D.W. Higgins, observed that, "Strange as it many seem, the class who showed the greatest objection to Negro equality were Northern men." These American northerners certainly made up the largest single group of foreigners in the colony, and if Higgins was right, their influence would have been considerable.

With the end of the Civil War in 1865, however, racial tension in Victoria dropped sharply. Many white Americans returned to the U.S. at about this time, since the colony's economy was slumping. To many Blacks as well, the U.S. was now even more attractive than Vancouver Island had been seven years earlier. Slavery was abolished and the Republican government was encouraging Black advancement. Contrarily in the British Northwest, the Blacks had seen steady erosion in their economic and political status. The increasing hypocrisy and pettiness of English-born Victorians must have been especially discouraging; with an American bigot, at least one knew where one stood. So the rapid departure of much of the Black community was understandable.

Now a shrinking minority, the Blacks were still relatively prosperous, but too few to have much political or social impact. As a result, public tolerance of them greatly increased, though private discrimination doubtlessly continued against them. They had originally come determined not to segregate themselves. With the disappearance of the circumstances that had forced them to create a bloc, they were able to live as they had intended.

CHAPTER ELEVEN

"The world is my country . . ."

In July of 1865, Schuyler Colfax, Speaker of the U.S. House of Representatives, paid a visit to Victoria. During his stay he met rather ceremoniously with Mifflin Gibbs and A.H. Francis. Gibbs did most of the talking.

"On being introduced by the American Consul," a newspaper account related, "Mr. Gibbs proceeded to say that they were happy to meet him and tender on behalf of the colored residents of Victoria their esteem and regard. They were not unacquainted with the noble course he had pursued during the great struggle in behalf of human liberty in the land of their nativity.... now that victory had perched upon the national standard — a standard henceforth and forever consecrated to universal liberty — they were filled with joy unspeakable."

There was more in such sentiments than mere rhetoric. The United States, which Gibbs had once termed a despotism, was now committed to freedom and equality for all Blacks. Those who had come as immigrants in 1858 were now beginning to feel like exiles. Some returned — in general, the less established, less successful Blacks. But many in the Black community had put down roots in the British Northwest, and had gained enough wealth to insulate themselves from white prejudice. There was no threat of persecution against the elite as there had been in California; Victoria's social climate had also improved. If whites' overtures had not increased, their provocations had at least lessened. The Victoria newspapers, which had once been filled with stories and letters on racial issues, now let months go by without mentioning the Blacks. The attention that they did receive—a benign paragraph or two about a 'Bachelors' Pic-Nic" or the annual Emancipation Day celebrations—contrasted pleasantly against such inflammatory accounts as that of the "Cary-Franklin Jollification" in 1860.

For Mifflin Gibbs, always eager for new challenges, Victoria must have been growing too safe and dull. In 1864 he had ended his long partnership with Peter Lester, and thereafter seems to have earned his living from real estate, construction, and investments. In November of 1866 he ran again for city council in his home ward of James Bay—the most affluent in the city—and was elected. His abilities were recognized by his colleagues on the council, and as chairman of the finance committee he wielded considerable influence. He even served for a time as acting mayor.

The year was a memorable one for Gibbs in another way as well. In seven years, Maria Gibbs had borne five children, one of whom had died. Now she took her children back to Oberlin, leaving Gibbs alone in Victoria. The reasons for this separation are unknown. But it may well have been that Gibbs was, as he later described himself, "a husband migratory and uncertain," always following some new enthusiasm. It is also likely that Maria had come to dislike Victoria; she was one of the best-educated women in the city, but her social life must have been limited since white women did not mix with Blacks.

Alone, Gibbs carried on with his usual energy, looking after his investments, conducting municipal business, and taking an active part in colonial politics. He was a well liked and respected figure, and a sought-after speaker. But, though he prospered in the colony, Gibbs was still in many ways an outsider, frustrated by the "old fogies" and their lack of "Yankee enterprise." One outlet for this frustration was a series of letters which he published in *The Elevator,* the Black San Francisco newspaper, during the spring and summer of 1868. In the first of these he praised the potential of British Columbia while damning its government:

"We have been badly governed.... hundreds of agriculturists seeking land to settle were treated with such nonchalance or charged such fabulous prices that they left...." Gibbs noted the gradual improvement of farming despite lack of government encouragement, and saw a bright future for mining: "We also have an an-

thracite mine which will be of great value not only to the owners
and to the colony, but to the Pacific coast, it being the only anthracite mine yet discovered on this side of the continent. The company (of which the writer has been a director) has spent $60,000
already...with a promise of excellent returns." The timber market
was also improving. "One year ago it was a difficult matter to in-
duce an intelligent shipmaster to load his vessel with lumber or
spars at Burrard Inlet; today seven large vessels are loading or preparing to load at the mills there...."

In his next letter, a month later, Gibbs praised English fairness
but bitterly attacked the government as "sitting like a nightmare
upon the energies of the people, and...totally unfitted for an intelligent community in the nineteenth century.... The Governor is
the personification of official imbecility.... We have a legislature...
which is but a sham."

What is more interesting than his description (which many British Columbians would have applied to every government from
Douglas to the present) is his remedy: "a cheap and responsible
government; to economize, by reducing it numerically, or by increasing its efficiency; to have a responsible government of the
people, for the people, and by the people." In other words, Gibbs
was now weighing the possibility of seeing British Columbia an-
nexed to the United States. In this he was allied with many Victoria businessmen, who for a time actively resisted the idea of
Confederation with the remote Canadian colonies. Like them,
Gibbs was an annexationist on economic grounds, but he took care
to praise the idea without committing himself to it personally.
"Annexation was quite popular with the masses," he wrote in *The
Elevator,* "but not with the colonial elite of government officials
and wealthy Englishmen whose support would be needed for such
a step." This was not entirely accurate; such Establishment figures
as John Sebastian Helmcken were very cool to Confederation and
willing at least to consider annexation as an option. Speaking for
himself, Gibbs said: "I have no very decided convictions of the
impropriety of territory changing ownership;...lands should be-
long to those who by the accident of locality or superior ability
can utilize it most efficiently and produce the greatest development."

But the annexation movement failed to win wide support, and
Gibbs saw Confederation as the only practical alternative. In his

last *Elevator* letter, written in July, Gibbs described the impending
union with Canada as a consequence of "the great principle of
national centralization and fraternity" which had united Germany
and was doing so in Italy. He scourged the Assembly for having
voted against Confederation for "the very human reason that they
were not fools enough to vote themselves out of office — thus pre-
senting in a nutshell the rottenness of the present system." And
after praising Confederation because it would end autocratic colonial government, Gibbs wrote:

"But to the new nation: Who shall write its rise, decline and
fall? Springing into existence almost in a day, with four million of
people, a population larger than the United States possessed when
they commenced their great career, who shall correctly predict its
future?

"That the banner of the Dominion and the stars and stripes,
linked and inter-linked, may go forward in healthful rivalry to
bless mankind and hasten the day when from pole to pole men
may exclaim, 'The world is my country and all mankind my countrymen!' is the sincere desire of the writer...."

In the fall, Gibbs was elected to represent Saltspring Island at
the Yale Convention, where terms for British Columbia's entry into
Canada were defined. The Convention was largely the work of
Amor De Cosmos, with whom Gibbs was evidently now on better
terms. While Gibbs's contribution to the convention is uncertain,
his presence was used by some to deride the cause of Confederation; a Victoria baker even concocted a sugar sculpture showing
a very black Gibbs arm-in-arm with a very drunk De Cosmos.

Such crude gibes could not stop Confederation, and racist appeals failed to keep Gibbs from being re-elected to the Victoria
City Council in 1868. He was a well known member of a minority
too small to be considered a threat; the 1868 census showed just
127 black adults in the Victoria district, whose white population
was 2,200.

Though Gibbs was an effective and conscientious councillor, he
was soon restless. The Queen Charlotte Coal Company, of which
he was both a director and a major shareholder, called for tenders
to build a wharf and tramway to serve its new mine; Gibbs resigned

his directorship and put in a bid, which was accepted though it was not the lowest one. In January 1869, he embarked for the Queen Charlottes on the steamship *Otter* with a crew of fifty workers: surveyors, carpenters, blacksmiths, and laborers. He had a three-month leave of absence from the city council, and expected to be back in Victoria in time for the opening of Victoria House, the largest and most modern mercantile building in the colony, which he had been constructing on one of his downtown lots.

The *Otter's* destination was a rough camp on Queen Charlotte Island, a few miles up the Skidegate River. The Haidas, despite their reputation for ferocity, gave the newcomers a friendly reception. "They were peaceful and docile," Gibbs later recalled, "lending ready hands to our landing and afterward to the cargo. I was surprised, while standing on the ship, to hear my name called by an Indian in a canoe at the side, coupled with encomiums of the native variety, quite flattering. It proved to be one who had been a domestic in my family at Victoria. He gave me kind welcome, not to be ignored, remembering that I was 'in the enemy's country,' so to speak."

Gibbs was careful to maintain good relations with the Haidas, on whom he relied for most of his work force. A decade earlier, Governor Douglas had complained of the unreliability of Indian workers, but Gibbs's experience with them was better: "While their work was despatched without celerity of trained labor, still, as is general with labor, they earned all they got...I found many apt, some stupid; honesty and dishonesty in usual quantities...."

Cultural differences did pose some difficulties. The original samples of coal had been carried down the slopes of Mount Seymour by Haida workers who were paid in tobacco for each bag of coal delivered on the ship. There had been no hurry then; but now, as work settled into a routine, the Haidas frequently went on strike — for more time, not more wages.

The workers who had come with Gibbs were of varied nationalities, and included three other Black men. For once, racial and national animosities were a benefit: each group disliked the others, but none was large enough to form a bloc that might slow down the work. Nevertheless, the work did go slowly. The men were hampered by almost constant rain, and by the effects of liquor. Gibbs found the engineering problems of the tramway more formidable than expected. From the mouth of the mine, the tramway ran a third of the distance down the mountain to a chute; the coal went down this chute to a second tramway, and thence to the wharf. Gibbs overcame the construction problems, but it took him months longer than planned.

Having outstayed his leave, Gibbs lost his councillor's seat; in July 1869, a cheerful and bigoted Irish brewer named Arthur Bunster replaced him on council. (This was the start of a long political career based on jokes and rabid anti-Chinese sentiments.) Gibbs had a stake in the mine's success, and little to draw him back to Victoria, so he agreed, after completing the tramway, to stay on as mine superintendent. He oversaw several shipments of anthracite, and handled the job as successfully as he had the tramway. But a mining camp on a remote island in the North Pacific was an unlikely place for a man of Gibbs's abilities, and in the spring of 1870 he returned to Victoria. He did not stay long. Though he held on to Victoria House, he liquidated his other interests and left to rejoin his family in Ohio.

"It was not without a measure of regret that I anticipated my departure," he wrote in his autobiography. "There I had lived more than a decade, where the geniality of the climate was excelled only by the graciousness of the people;...there I had received social and political recognition; there my domestic ties had been intensified by the birth of my children.... Then regret modified, as love of home and country asserted itself."

This was characteristic of Gibbs: to fight battles and forget them. Privately, he may have nursed resentments, but publicly he expressed himself with considerable tact. Unfortunately, Gibbs maintained that tact in discussing his political status: "I had left politically ignoble; I was returning panoplied with the nobility of an American citizen." But he had become a naturalized British subject in 1861, and it is unclear how his American citizenship was obtained.

In Oberlin, Gibbs was briefly reunited with his family while he studied law at Tanner's Commercial College, a private business school; he did not, as many accounts claim, enrol at Oberlin College. He had read English common law in Victoria under D.B. Ring, and was graduated from Tanner's in less than a year. He then left Ohio, planning to settle somewhere in the south. It was no small achievement for a man nearing 50 to embark on a new career in unfamiliar country.

His first stop was Tallahassee, Florida, where his brother Jonathan — a Dartmouth graduate — was Secretary of State. White resistance to Black participation in government was already well organized; to sleep, Jonathan Gibbs had to climb to the attic of his large home and surround himself with a small arsenal in anticipation of raids by the new Ku Klux Klan. Though encouraged to settle in Florida, Gibbs felt that to do so would be taking advantage of his brother's position. He moved on. In 1871 he entered a law firm in Little Rock, Arkansas; a year later, he opened his own firm. Once settled, he seems to have been reunited with his wife, at least for awhile.

Success in Gibbs's new profession came swiftly. In 1873, he became the first Black man in the U.S. to be elected municipal judge — and by a predominantly white electorate. He also became an important figure in the state Republican party, and was a delegate to most of the Republican presidential conventions for the rest of the century. After Reconstruction, a Black Republican in a southern state ran some risks. Years later, he told an interviewer in Los Angeles that he had sometimes "stumped the state" when hostilities were so intense that "my wife never expected to see me again, and I saw my fellow-men shot down by hot-headed Democrats, who tried to break up the meetings." His loyalty was sometimes more than the party deserved; in 1876 he was one of the 306 convention delegates who tried to nominate Ulysses S. Grant for a third term as president. But Republican administrations rewarded him with several important posts, including Registrar of the U.S. Land Office for Little Rock, and Receiver of Public Money; he filled these quite ably.

In 1897, Gibbs was appointed U.S. Consul for Madagascar. Surprised and excited, he accepted the post and embarked on New Year's Day, 1898; after a month's stay in Paris, he continued his journey and arrived at Tamatave — a small coastal town — in mid-February. He was just two months short of his 75th birthday; he would be nearly 78 when he left. For over three years, Gibbs lived in that remote tropical backwater, becoming a popular and respected member of the small foreign community. The climate was brutal; bubonic plague and "Malagash fever" were seasonal

hazards. When he returned home in 1901, it was with some eager-
ness.

His next project was the writing of *Shadow and Light*, which
was privately published in Washington, D.C., in 1902. In Little
Rock again, he became the president of Capital City Savings Bank,
most of whose depositors were Black people. The position gave him
time for considerable travel, and in 1907 he visited Victoria. A
story in the *Colonist* described him as a Democrat and got several
other facts wrong, but this was getting off lightly after the days of
De Cosmos's race-baiting.

On 11 July 1915, at the age of 92, Mifflin Wistar Gibbs died.
Little Rock's new Black high school had been named for him. He
had given the land for a home for aged Black women, and had
supported the home with sizable donations. "He leaves a large estate," the Little Rock *Gazette* noted in his obituary.

Little is known about his family. Maria Gibbs was already dead;
so was their son Donald, who had returned to Victoria sometime
in the 1880s. Gibbs's other son, Horace, was a printer in Aurora,
Illinois; Hattie Gibbs Marshall, after graduating from the Conser-
vatory of Music at Oberlin, became a musical director of the public schools in Washington, D.C.; her sister, Ida Alexander Hunt,
taught English in those schools, but was living in St. Etrenne,
France, when Gibbs died.

Nor is much known about most of the Blacks who returned to
the United States. It is recorded that John Craven Jones, Saltspring's
first teacher, also returned to Oberlin in the mid-1870s. In 1882,
at the age of 51, he married Almira Scott (who had graduated
from Oberlin in 1870), and moved to Tarboro, North Carolina,
where he taught for the next twenty-five years. One source claims
he also became a lawyer. In 1911, four years after retiring from
teaching, Jones died of blood poisoning in Greensboro, N.C.

Jones and the Gibbs family must surely have known each other in
Oberlin, if not in British Columbia. One wonders how they recalled
their years in the Northwest: did they see their sojourn as a mistake, an adventure, an experiment that failed? As Reconstruction
ended and white supremacy was restored, did they ever wish they
had stayed in the "God-sent land for the colored people"?

The departure of Mifflin Gibbs marked a turning point in the history of the Blacks of British Columbia. He had been widely regarded as the leader of a distinct community, with its own interests and the political power to pursue them. Now the leader was gone and the community's nature was radically changed. Many of the immigrants of 1858 had left long before Gibbs. There had been, in the early 1860s, perhaps eight hundred to a thousand Blacks in the British Northwest. The 1871 Victoria Directory numbered just 439 Blacks (many of them children) in the whole of the new province of British Columbia, not counting Saltspring Island's estimated ten Black families.

The white and Chinese populations, meanwhile, had been growing fairly steadily. White dislike of Orientals had always been strong, and increased throughout the rest of the century. The Blacks were no longer much noticed; when they were, they were seen as natural allies of the whites. James Morton, in his history of the Chinese in British Columbia, quotes a *Colonist* editorial of 1875 that rebuked a city councillor for saying that the Chinese ought to be able to vote since Blacks already could: "Colored persons differ only from the white in point of color," the editorial asserted. "In language, religion, habits of life, and thought, they are the same. They are not less intelligent, enterprising, industrious, orderly, benevolent. They own as much property, pay as much taxes. In a word, they are no less citizens and no less capable of making good use of the electoral franchise on account of their color. But in all these respects the Chinese are essentially different and are likely to remain so...they are precisely the element to be desired and used at an election by the designing and unscrupulous." No doubt some Black readers grinned wryly at this accolade, remembering Amor De Cosmos's use of the same arguments during the 1860 election.

In effect, the Blacks had suffered what might be called a "Pyrrhic defeat." They had lost their influence as the balance of power between establishment and reform factions; they had endured insults and discrimination while the government they had supported looked the other way; they had seen some of their most enterprising people return to the United States. But they had come in

1858 intending to integrate themselves, not to found still another ghetto. For those who remained, that integration was now in many respects achieved. They would still encounter prejudice, but not of the sort they had faced in the early 1860s. They sat where they chose in the theaters, voted as they saw fit in the elections, and generally carried on their lives as individuals. And as individuals they continued to make notable contributions to British Columbia in its first decades as a Canadian province.

One man who did much to open up the far northwest of the province was a Black prospector named Henry McDame. According to an anonymous article in *Canada West Magazine,* McDame was a native of the Bahamas who came to B.C. in 1858 and spent an uneventful decade prospecting in the Cariboo. Then, in 1870, he was one of four men who discovered a rich gold creek in the Omineca. Four years later he pushed on into the Cassiar wilderness; ninety miles from Dease Lake he found gold again. To exploit the claim, McDame and several other miners — most of them Black — formed the Charity Company, which took out six thousand dollars' worth of gold in its first month of operations. The stream on which the "Discovery Claim" was located was first known as "Nigger Creek," but was later named for McDame. A decade later, in 1884, McDame was exploring the Skeena district with a grubstake from Samuel Booth, a prosperous Victoria Black. Here he found several gold-bearing streams, most notably Lorne Creek. What became of him afterward is uncertain; a photograph of "old timers" taken in Telegraph Creek in 1897 includes a Black man who may have been Henry McDame. Whatever his personal successes were, McDame deserves recognition as one of the prospectors who first penetrated B.C.'s remotest frontiers.

One of McDame's partners in the Omineca had been Daniel Williams, very likely the same Daniel Williams who became a legend in the Peace River country. Born in Ontario, Williams came west in 1857 as a cook with the Palliser Expedition. He decided to stay, and became a successful trapper and prospector. In 1869 Williams became the first settler at Fort St. John, a Hudson's Bay post; from this base he traveled widely across little-known country. His quarrels with the HBC at Fort St. John lasted for years; he disliked chasing the traders' livestock out of his vegetable garden, and was outraged when the company claimed his farm as part of its property. Williams was also the first to grow wheat in the Peace River country, a region then considered hopeless for agriculture; he proved the opposite.

Thanks to his prickly personality, Williams gained a reputation as a dangerous man, one who had even got away with murder. On one occasion he shot at the HBC trader at Fort St. John and was tried on a charge of "causing a disturbance." A fellow-miner known as Banjo Mike conducted Williams's defense. James G. McGregor, in his book *The Land of Twelve Foot Davis,* tells the story well: "Banjo Mike was able to prove that Dan was only a short distance from McKinley when he fired at him. Having established this point, Mike turned triumphantly to the jury and said: 'Gentlemen, let me tell you this: I know, as many other miners know, that Dan Williams at a distance of one hundred yards can take the eye out of a jackrabbit at every pop. Well, gentlemen, had Dan Williams had the slightest intention of harming Mr. Mc-Kinley, Mr. McKinley would not be here to tell you this amusing little story, whereby he gives you credit for some sense of humor without paying you much of a compliment for intelligence." According to McGregor, Williams's sentence was greatly reduced thanks to this argument.

Williams returned to the Peace River after his release from jail. Some sources believe he was the Black man named Williams who was hanged for murder in Calgary in 1884, but it seems more likely that he died in 1887 while wintering on the Finlay River — perhaps of illness, perhaps murdered by his partner.

Most of the province's Blacks continued to live in and around Victoria, pursuing careers somewhat less spectacular than Williams's. T.W. Pierre was a successful tailor; Richard Stokes kept a livery stable. James Barnswell, a Jamaican, became a prominent member of the community during the 1870s. Born in 1829, he arrived in Victoria during the gold-rush years and established himself as a carpenter, building some of Victoria's most elegant homes. In 1871 he married Mary Lowe, who had been born in Puerto Rico in 1853 and who arrived in B.C. as an orphaned teenager speaking only Spanish. The Barnswells had ten children, some of whose descendants still live in the province. Barnswell died in 1919 at the age of 90; his wife, who was widely known and respected in both Black and white communities for her intelligence, common sense, and integrity, died in 1947 at 95. Robert Clanton, an Ohio-born baker, was another well known figure. In 1866 he married Victoria Richard — almost certainly the daughter of Fortune Richard — and founded a family to whom many modern B.C. Blacks are related.

If Daniel Williams was the archetypal backwoodsman, solitary and stubborn, Charles Alexander was the frontier patriarch. Born in St. Louis, Missouri, in 1824, Alexander was the son of a Black mother and an Indian father. Like his wife, Nancy, he was born free. After their marriage in 1849, they lived in St. Louis until 1857, when they moved to California. Arriving at the peak of anti-Black feeling, the Alexanders soon went on to Victoria as part of the emigration of 1858. While his wife stayed in Victoria, Charles Alexander went to the gold fields of the Fraser, where he did well as a miner. In 1861 he rejoined his family and bought land at Shady Creek, in the Saanich district north of Victoria. He soon became a prominent and respected farmer.

Alexander helped to build Shady Creek Methodist Church in the early 1860s, on land owned by a Black man named McMillan. For some years the church had no regular minister, but Alexander himself frequently preached there. George Glover, in his history of the United Church in the Saanich area, gives us a description of Alexander that matches his photograph: "He stood six feet two inches and weighed over 200 pounds, with broad shoulders and a deep, splendid voice for both singing and speaking. His great, broad hands gripped in a most friendly greeting and that grip was never forgotten. In his way he was a Bible scholar and a most interesting and capable teacher and preacher. He was one of the group most anxious to have a church in the community and gave much of his time and ability as a carpenter to help in this purpose."

Alexander also served as a school trustee, helped to build the first schoolhouse in South Saanich, and was a founding member of the local agricultural and temperance societies. After his retirement from farming, he and his wife moved to Lake Hill; it was there that most of their large family gathered on Christmas Day

1899 to celebrate the Alexanders' golden anniversary. The *Colonist* reported the event at some length:

"Golden Wedding — Unusual celebration held at Lake Hill — On Christmas Day, Mr. and Mrs. Charles Alexander of Lake Hill, formerly of Saanich, were married in 1849 in Springfield, Illinois. Twelve children were born to them, of whom seven are still living, and besides they have 21 grandchildren. With the exception of one daughter, all were present at the celebration...." Some of the oldest families in the province were also there: the Dallas Helmckens, the Tolmies, the Howards, and the Shakespeares. Among the Black guests were Robert and Victoria Clanton; Mrs. Charles Spotts; Mrs. T.W. Pierre; and James and Mary Barnswell — all of whom had come to Vancouver Island in the gold-rush years.

Charles Alexander died in 1913 at the age of 89, and was buried in the Shady Creek cemetery beside his wife, who had died two years earlier. In the early 1900s the Alexander family ran a successful coal business in Victoria and one Victorian recalls that the men in the business were all capable of carrying sacks of coal weighing over 200 pounds. Many of the Alexanders' descendants still live in British Columbia, where they are active in business, the professions, and education; one of them, Norman Alexander, is a former president of the B.C. Association for the Advancement of Colored People.

The Spotts family, who were represented at the Alexanders' celebration, had been well known in B.C. for years. Fielding Spotts arrived from California in 1859, and a year later brought his wife Julia and their son, Fielding William, to join him. The family farmed on Saltspring Island for a few years, but eventually moved to Saanich. Spotts, like Alexander, served for many years as a school trustee. The family's eight children were well liked, and several were renowned local athletes. Fielding William moved to Vancouver in 1902; he died in 1937, one of the last of the original pioneers.

One veteran of Victoria's first police force, Lorne Lewis, made a career of law enforcement. According to William Daniel Anderson, who was born in 1856 and reared on Saltspring Island, Lewis served for years as a district constable on the Songhees Indian Reserve outside Victoria; he later became a member of the Provincial Police, as did Anderson himself. Lewis evidently did some farming as well, and was on the South Saanich voters' list until 1877.

A Black businessman named John Sullivan Deas gained some prominence on the Lower Mainland during the 1870s; thanks to the research of H. Keith Ralston, a UBC historian, we now know about Deas's career in some detail. Deas was born in South Carolina in the late 1830s, and became a tinsmith while still in his teens. By 1860 he was working in San Francisco, and in 1862 he moved to Vancouver Island, where he married Fanny Harris that same year. The wedding took place in the home of Richard H. Johnson, a VPRC officer and later the builder of the Hotel Ararat during the Sooke gold rush.

Deas moved to Yale for a couple of years during the mid-1860s, but by 1868 he was back in Victoria as the proprietor of Birmingham House, a hardware and stove business. In 1871, he and his family moved into Richard Johnson's house, Johnson having recently died. The new tenants were the victims of a prank : another Black, carrying a "bull's-eye" lantern, came up to one of the windows on the family's first night in the house, and so frightened them that they moved out the next morning. The "haunting" caused a brief sensation in Victoria until the truth came out a few days later.

In that same year, Deas contracted with Captain Edward Stamp to make the cans for Stamp's new salmon-cannery venture in New Westminster — one of the first in British Columbia. Stamp died in England soon after, while trying to raise more capital, but with backing from a Victoria merchant firm Deas was able to go on canning. In 1873 he pre-empted the island in the Fraser Delta that now bears his name, and built a sizable complex of buildings that served as cannery, warehouse, and bunkhouse. Here he began packing salmon in cans lithographed for him by Grafton T. Brown, a Black artist in San Francisco. For several years, Deas contended with uncertain salmon runs and technological problems. In 1872 and 1873, he nevertheless packed twice as much salmon as any of the growing number of his competitors. Aware that the river could not sustain operations on the scale of the Columbia River canneries, Deas watched the increasing competition with some foreboding. In 1877, the owners of a rival cannery charged him with using "violent and threatening" language to their fishermen. The case was thrown out of court, but not before Deas had been put to the inconvenience of appealing a three-week jail sentence. The *Mainland Guardian* observed that the whole matter was obviously intended to interfere with Deas's operations at the height of the canning season.

Such tactics helped to end Deas's career in the new industry. His output fell from first to third place in 1877, and as still more canneries were being set up for the 1878 season, he saw little point in remaining. Late in 1877, his wife bought a rooming house in Portland, Oregon. After working through the peak of the 1878 season, Deas sold out to his Victoria backers for an estimated $15,000, and after clearing up his affairs he joined his family in Portland. Two years later he died at the age of 42; as Ralston observes, tinsmithing was a notoriously unhealthful trade, and Deas's early death may have been related to his work. It is one of the many ironies of the Blacks' experience in British Columbia that John Sullivan Deas — a pioneer in one of the province's major industries — is today known only because a major highway goes under the Fraser through what for years was named the Deas Island Tunnel.

Willis Bond, the popular orator and house-mover, went on enjoying controversy. In 1886, he attended an anti-Chinese rally in Victoria at which only he and Victoria's mayor, James Fell, spoke against a resolution calling for deportation of all Chinese in the province. The audience shouted him down, but one suspects that Bond was delighted to see he could still stir up his opponents. He died in Victoria in 1892. D.W. Higgins, once Speaker of the provincial legislature, called Bond "the cleverest man, black or white, I ever knew."

Wellington Moses settled permanently in Barkerville, a well known and beloved old-timer. Though he seems to have had no children of his own, the children of Barkerville often got presents from him at Christmas: toy trumpets, slates, tea sets and dolls. In 1875, he recorded the burial of six-year-old John Kelly in nearby Camerontown; though he did not express his feelings about it, no doubt he shared the parents' sorrow.

Fortune Richard, one of the original Pioneer Committee, took little part in public life after the disbanding of the African Rifles. But in 1882 he published a protest against a faction in Victoria's

Baptist Church which, under pretext of financial distress, was trying to get rid of its Black members.

Most of the Stark family moved from Saltspring to a new farm,
called the Extension, in Nanaimo's Cranberry District. In the 1890s,
a rich coal seam was found to run through the property, and Louis
Stark received urgent offers to buy his land. He refused. Some of
the would-be buyers threatened him, but Stark was unmoved.
Then, in 1895, he was found dead at the bottom of a cliff. Though
murder could not be proven, the family was convinced that he
had been killed. According to one account, Louis's brother John —
a noted prospector who was the co-discoverer of the Dolly Varden
mine in the Yukon — tried to investigate the death, but was himself
threatened and even shot at. Sylvia and her children continued to
live on the Extension for some years, but mining did go on under
their property; they could often hear the blasting underground.

Eventually Sylvia returned to Saltspring, where her oldest son,
Willis, had been running Fruitvale. As a toddler he had been kept
indoors for fear of cougars; as a man, he was a famous hunter of
them. The Starks' oldest daughter, Emma, became a schoolteacher while still in her teens, and worked for many years on
Vancouver Island in the 1870s and 1880s. Sylvia Stark was to live
to the age of 106; she died in 1944, her memory still sharp and
her storytelling as vivid as ever.

A few Blacks continued to drift into the province. One of these
was John Freemont Smith; a native of the Danish West Indies
(now the Virgin Islands), Smith was a restless, multi-talented man
whose career was much like that of Mifflin Gibbs. After some years
in Victoria, where he married in 1877, Smith opened a shoemaker's shop in Kamloops in 1884. In 1886, he moved to nearby
Louis Creek, and later like to boast wryly that he was "the first
white man on the North Thompson." For several years Smith prospected all over the B.C. interior, and tried unsuccessfully to develop some mica deposits at Tête Jaune Cache; he was also involved
in a coal-mining venture at Chu Chua. In 1898 Smith and his
family returned to Kamloops, where he set up a store and also
worked as a mining and agriculture journalist. In 1902 he became
secretary of the local Board of Trade; a year later he was elected

alderman, a post he held for four years. Smith's career as a prospector, businessman, and Indian agent seems to have been notably untouched by prejudice. He was a popular community leader, respected for his energetic "boosting" of Kamloops.

In one of his letters, Mifflin Gibbs had commented on the growing industry on Burrard Inlet; by the mid-1870s, Blacks were taking part in that growth. Philip Sullivan, a steward at Moody's Mill, was perhaps the first Black resident of what was to become North Vancouver. His son, Arthur W. Sullivan, was one of the first merchants in "Granville" — better known as Gastown and later as Vancouver. Described in a 1929 *Province* article as "a colored man of pale complexion and delicate features," Sullivan ran a grocery store on Water Street at least as early as 1876. He was also a musician, and played the organ at services in the Methodist Hall across the street. His wife, Josephine, was an active leader of the small Methodist congregation. Their business was destroyed in the fire of 1886, but was soon re-established in a new building known as the Sullivan Block.

A Barbadian named Seraphim Fortes arrived in Vancouver in 1885. After working for several years as a porter and bartender, he established himself in a little shack on English Bay just south of Stanley Park. According to Alan Morley, "Joe" Fortes became the virtual proprietor of the beach: "...Scarcely a tyke who was raised in Vancouver in the '90's or 1900's but learned to swim with Joe's hamlike fist gripping the back of his or her cotton bathing suit.... how many lives he saved over the years will never be known, but he has been credited with over one hundred witnessed rescues, some of them in desperate circumstances. When — as was bound occasionally to happen — his utmost efforts failed, his grief was shattering to behold. Mothers confidently shooed their children away to the bay for the long summer days with the simple command '...and don't go away from where Joe is.'"

Those children learned that Joe Fortes was a skilled teacher but also a stern custodian of the beach. William C. Heilbron recalled in 1961 a 1900 episode in which he and seven or eight other boys "highjacked" a steam launch and set out on a cruise of English Bay. Joe overtook them in his rowboat. "Each of the crew, according to rank, got spanked, and hard, by Joe in the places it hurt the worst, and he didn't mention a word of our delinquency to parents.... He wasn't hard boiled in the least, he just understood kids."

Originally a squatter who lived by odd jobs while informally acting as swimming teacher and lifeguard, Fortes was eventually appointed officially; he was also made a special constable. When he died of pneumonia in 1922, the city arranged a public funeral which was attended by hundreds. A few years later his abandoned cottage was burned down, but à more permanent memorial still stands — a fountain-monument with a bronze plaque inscribed: "Little children loved him."

Despite the fame of a few individuals like Joe Fortes, Black people by the turn of the century were so thinly scattered across the province that they rarely came to public notice. In 1899, a man named Archibald Johnson protested the refusal of some Victoria barbers to cut Black men's hair; it was practically the only Black-related item to appear that year, except for the Alexanders' golden anniversary.

The children and grandchildren of the pioneers acquired a certain reserve in their relations with whites. Mrs. Nan E. Tremayne, who attended Victoria High School from 1903 to 1906, recalls the mixture of friendliness and distance between her family and a branch of the Alexanders: "One of my classmates was a Black girl named Wealtha Alexander, who was well-liked by everyone, though never one of any particular group. Her mother was an excellent dressmaker and made dresses for a lot of well-known women, and of course her daughter was always well turned out. Her father was the owner-driver of a dray for whom my father, in the Customs service, had a lot of respect...but he was always kept at a respectful distance, and I *think* I would not have been allowed to bring the daughter into our home. Nor would she have wanted to come." If this was a typical attitude, it indicates that the Blacks had — after almost half a century's contribution to the province — gained little more than tolerance. They faced far less institutional discrimination than most American Blacks, but that was due to their fewness, not to their fellow-citizens' enlightenment.

In any case, the anxieties of the white community were now firmly focused on the Asians — the Chinese, Japanese, and East Indians — whose numbers, energy, and foreignness thoroughly alarmed all classes of British Columbia society. As with the Blacks

forty years before, it was charged that the Asians were "unass
able," holding attitudes and values too alien to permit them an
equal position in a white man's country. In fact, the Asians were—
like the Blacks—disliked because their attitudes and values were
thoroughly appropriate to a developing and fiercely competitive
economy. They worked harder and longer, for less pay, than their
white neighbors cared to. They saved their money and invested it
wisely; they sacrificed to educate their children. If, like some of
the Chinese, they came to B.C. only to build up a stake to take
back home, they were no different in this than thousands of white
prospectors had been in 1858.

The story of the Black pioneers in British Columbia began with
an act of violence in a San Francisco boot shop; perhaps it may be
said to have ended fifty years later, in another act of violence. In
September 1907, a meeting in Vancouver of the Asiatic Exclusion
League (at which a number of clergymen and community leaders
were honored to speak) led to an attack on Chinatown by a white
mob. The race riot paralyzed the city—indeed, the whole province—for days, and caused serious international repercussions.
After almost a week of battles, strikes, and random violence, a
white man named McGregor wandered off Pender Street into
Canton Alley, where several Chinese were cutting wood. According to one account, he did nothing but casually kick at a piece
of wood; according to another, he was drunk, and assaulted one
of the Chinese. What is certain is that he was set upon by as many
as thirty Chinese, and seriously stabbed in the head and face; a
crowd of whites on Pender Street stood by and watched.

Before the white could be killed, one person went into the mob
in Canton Alley and rescued him. She was a Black woman—"a
colored woman of the half-world," the Vancouver *Province* called
her, who "jumped into the fray and managed to get McGregor
into a door where she protected him from his assailants until the
arrival of the police."

Who she was is unknown. But, like all the Blacks of British
Columbia, she was in her way a teacher. Many of us have yet to
learn what they taught.

EPILOGUE

". . . and all mankind my countrymen."

L ike the pioneers, the modern Blacks of British Columbia have contributed more to the larger society than their numbers would seem to warrant, and without gaining the recognition they deserve. While they may have suffered less overt discrimination than their American cousins, they have not escaped it completely; the war of complexional distinction is not yet over for them, or for their fellow-citizens of all races. Though a detailed history of the Blacks in modern B.C. is beyond the scope of this book, the outlines of that history can be traced.

In the last years of the nineteenth century, one or two Blacks tried unsuccessfully to promote renewed Black immigration to British Columbia. Around the turn of the century, however, numbers of Blacks from Oklahoma came through Vancouver en route to homesteads in Alberta — despite Ottawa's strenuous efforts to frustrate such migration. Some of these settlers, along with Blacks from eastern Canada, eventually moved into British Columbia. At the same time, at least a few B.C. Blacks moved to the United States, usually for economic reasons. The province's Black population therefore grew little, if at all, during the early 1900s.

As British Columbia's center of economic gravity shifted from Victoria to Vancouver, many Blacks moved to the Lower Mainland, and by 1900 they were numerous enough to hold a large and lively Emancipation Day celebration in North Vancouver's Moodyville. A *Province* reporter covered the event and described the participants in the usual racist cliches ("dusky maidens...a squash-face coon"), but was honest enough to note that the only disturbances at the event were caused by drunken whites.

A small Black community developed in the Strathcona district of Vancouver's East End; its focus was the Fountain Chapel A.M.E. Church on Jackson Street. Founded in 1908, the Church was active until the mid-1950s, though by World War II it was suffering from dwindling congregations and a rapid turnover of ministers — almost all of them Americans. But even this community, which by 1914 probably numbered no more than 300, was scattered, and its members seem to have felt little need for collective organization outside the church. According to Robin Winks, a Negro Christian Alliance was formed in Vancouver not long before World War I. Under its president, Milton Fuller, it tried to fight community prejudice, but with what success local history does not say.

Though World War I made enormous demands on Canada's manpower, Ottawa did not feel democracy quite threatened enough to warrant recruiting Blacks for combat duty. Contradictory policies were followed in the first years of the war: while no official barriers were placed in the way of Black volunteers, local commanders could reject them if they wished; most did. At least one B.C. unit accepted Blacks, however, for Leo Smith — the sole surviving son of John Freemont Smith — went overseas and was killed in action in 1918. But the great majority of Blacks who volunteered for service were assigned to construction and forestry units.

Probably the single most important nonreligious Black institution in B.C. in the early years of the century was the union of porters employed by the Canadian Pacific and Canadian National railways. Organized in 1919, it later amalgamated with the Americans as the Brotherhood of Sleeping Car Porters. Many of its members, born elsewhere, settled in Vancouver because it was the Canadian rail terminus. Through their occupation and their connections with the Brotherhood in the United States, members were in close touch with larger Black communities elsewhere in North America; as a result, Vancouver's Blacks were aware of, and influenced by, such movements as Marcus Garvey's United Negro Improvement Association, which flourished in the 1920s. A Garveyite group was established in Vancouver, and devoted most of its energies to encouraging young Blacks to become teachers and nurses. That such encouragement was considered neces-

sary is an indication that B.C. Blacks had lost some ground since
the 1860s and 1870s, when their status had been predominantly
middle-class and their children had been well educated as a matter of course.

In general, Black organizations seem to have made less public
impact on B.C. in the 1920s and 1930s than Black individuals
did. Until his death in 1922, Joe Fortes was the best known Black
in Vancouver, thanks to his position as lifeguard and special constable at English Bay Beach. Mary Barnswell, despite her lack of
formal education, was sought out by Victoria businessmen and
politicians who valued her intelligence and sound judgment. John
Freemont Smith continued to be active in Kamloops in 1934 at the
age of 83; he had just finished an article for the Kamloops *Sentinel*
the day before he died in his office in the Freemont block. George
Paris, a noted athlete who arrived in B.C. in 1899, had a long
career as a coach and trainer for boxers and runners; at the age
of 60, he became athletic coach for the Vancouver Police, a position he held until he was well past 75. Jay Mack McAdow, better
known as "Johnny Mack," settled in Vancouver in 1910; four years
later he organized the Independent Colored Political Association
to encourage Blacks to become naturalized and to educate them
politically. The ICPO endured for a quarter-century under Johnny
Mack's leadership as a consistent supporter of the Liberals and of
the municipal Non-Partisan Association. And in the northern Interior, a Virginia-born Black named Arthur Clore began a long,
legendary career as a prospector in 1910; the Clore River and Clore
Mountain are named for him. A tough, self-reliant bachelor, he
farmed and prospected successfully even through the Depression,
and was reluctant to accept help from anyone. "They tell me I
should collect the old age pension," he told an interviewer in the
1960s, "but I don't know if I will. I've stood on my own two feet
so long that it's hard to hold out your hand for something."
Young Blacks growing up in the years after World War I did
not encounter much discrimination, and were ill prepared for it
when they did. Earl Barnswell recalls being barred from a Victoria
swimming pool when he was about twelve — an incident that left a
lasting hurt. And in a case reminiscent of the 1860s, a Vancouver

shoemaker named Ed Rogers was refused service in a downtown hotel beer parlor in 1938. He went to court and was awarded damages, but not until two years later. The casual, almost random nature of such incidents made them especially hard to fight; they may have contributed to the tendency of B.C. Blacks to avoid much public involvement and to focus their energies on work and family. Those who grew up in the decades between the wars still remember the warmth and intensity of family ties. Indeed, descendants of many pioneers tended to marry each other. Much of the modern Black community belongs to one vast extended family as a result.

In the 1920s, the Ku Klux Klan established itself in British Columbia, though how firmly is uncertain: the Klan claimed a membership of ten thousand in B.C., and five MLAs were allegedly members in 1925. In that year an American Klan official was refused permission to enter B.C. from Washington, but a KKK meeting a few days later attracted two thousand people to the Hotel Vancouver. Lacking adequate Black targets, the B.C. Klan fell back on anti-Oriental agitation. In the late 1920s, a Vancouver Klan parade drew only two hundred marchers, most of them Americans; the KKK then rapidly collapsed through internal quarrels. Significantly, the Black community seems to have taken no overt steps against the Klan. Their strategy was wise, since an open attack would have given their enemies an issue.

In her novel *A Proper Marriage,* Doris Lessing describes a British colony in Africa which, at the outbreak of World War II, exhorts its Black population to join with the whites in fighting "the monster across the seas...whose crimes consisted of invading other people's countries and forming a society based on the conception of a master race." If the irony was less apparent in Canada than in Africa, it was still there for many racial minorities, including Blacks, Japanese, and native Indians. Color lines still existed in the armed forces, though they were drawn less firmly: Earl Barnswell was rejected by the Navy solely on grounds of his race, but was accepted by the Army. Descendants of other pioneer families also served; Rod Alexander, Charles Winchester, Bob Whims, and Tommy Woods were among them.

As in the United States, the war accelerated the pace of social change, and made British Columbia's Blacks as determined as their American cousins to make their country live up to its wartime egalitarian propaganda. One victory was the end of the ban on nonwhite use of the Crystal Pool near Stanley Park — a ban all the more outrageous in the park where Joe Fortes had taught a whole generation of white children how to swim.

Hotel discrimination had been an issue in Vancouver at least since 1909, when heavyweight boxing champion Jack Johnson and his wife had been denied lodgings at several hotels during their visit to the city. After World War II, such discrimination weakened under the pressure of increasing publicity. A touring company of *Carmen Jones* was alleged to have had difficulty finding accommodations in Vancouver; Black jazz groups such as the Jimmy Lunceford band had the same problem. But there were few reported incidents after the 1940s.

B.C. Blacks no doubt encountered similar problems in finding housing, but rarely publicized them. An exception was in 1948, when Dermont Cromwell, a Winnipeg-born chemical engineer, received threatening letters warning him and his family to get out of their home in southeast Vancouver. Cromwell got the issue onto the front pages of the *Sun* and *Province,* and the resulting publicity put an end to the threats.

Harder to combat was job discrimination. Cromwell, now the president of the Canadian Association for the Advancement of Colored People, charged in 1949 that Blacks in B.C. were largely consigned to a few occupations thanks to employers' ignorance. "If they'd try hiring some of us," he said, "they'd get a different viewpoint." William J. McLaughlin, business agent of the Brotherhood of Sleeping Car Porters, made the same point a few months later, accusing both businessmen and municipal employers of anti-Black discrimination.

What little information is available on Black employment in this period tends to confirm the view that Blacks were largely confined to such occupations as barbering, cooking, and semiskilled work. It is true that Edward Boynton worked for many years in the Vancouver city works department, and his brother Orville was a manager in the lumber industry until he retired at 80 in 1947, but they do not seem to have had many Black fellow-workers. Nevertheless, significant changes were already developing as a new generation began graduating from universities in B.C. and elsewhere and began entering the professions.

Though they might have made a considerable contribution to improving the status of British Columbia's Blacks in the 1940s, the province's media paid little attention aside from covering discrimination incidents here and there, and running an occasional human-interest story. In 1946, for example, the *Province* ran a story on Jim Anderson, the son of a pioneer Saltspring family. Though she described Anderson in admiring terms, the author of the story saw nothing wrong in describing him as a "darky." Other accounts tended to dwell on the more sensational aspects of Black history in B.C. —the tragedies of the Stark family, the theater "riot" of 1861, and so forth. One account hinted that Black farmers had murdered a Black cattle rustler on Saltspring. Not a scrap of evidence was offered for the story. And while some stories did deal with important persons and events, they generally portrayed the Black presence in B.C. as a minor curiosity of the province's early days, and often perpetuated such myths as that of Saltspring's Black "colony."

As the U.S. civil-rights movement gained momentum in the 1950s, however, British Columbia's newspapers began to mature in their treatment of local stories relating to Blacks. In 1954, they gave prominent and sympathetic coverage to the case of Dorothy Hewitt, the Jamaican bride of a white English teacher at Shawnigan Lake Boys' School; a week before classes began, the headmaster ordered her to leave the prestigious private school "before the boys come and see a colored person here." Mrs. Hewitt returned to Jamaica; the headmaster declined comment.

As we have seen, British Columbia's Blacks rarely formed racially oriented organizations except in the face of a specific threat, and such groups were usually short-lived. A break with this pattern was made in 1958 with the founding of the B.C. Association for the Advancement of Colored People. If its organizers —who included Frank Collins, Emmitt Holmes, and Howard Fair —perceived a threat, it was a subtle one: Blacks were going through rapid and profound change in B.C. as elsewhere, but they lacked adequate communication with each other and with the white community. The BCAACP set out to correct this problem.

From its inception, the Association was involved in both long-
and short-term activities. A Black community had first to be identified and described, both for itself and for the larger society.
Widespread ignorance and prejudice had to be replaced with knowledge and understanding, and racism had to be fought. Self-
definition began in 1958 with the compilation of a list of 250 Blacks
in B.C.; a year later, the "census" was expanded to 950. The Association set up links with similar groups in Alberta and the United
States; though it took its name from the Americans' NAACP, the
B.C. group remained independent. In 1961 Emancipation Day was
revived as a day of celebration. In the mid-1960s, the BCAACP
supported Martin Luther King's demonstrations in Selma, Ala-
bama; a few years later, it gave help to West Indian students involved in protests at Sir George Williams University in Montreal;
in the early 1970s it raised money for African drought relief. Intentionally or not, the Association found itself affirming Mifflin
Gibbs's vision of "the world my country, and all mankind my
countrymen." Though few in numbers, the Blacks of British Columbia were aware that they formed part of an immense, complex,
world-wide community which was itself still searching for a new
identity.

The BCAACP also set out to educate both its members and the
public. Its efforts included a study group on South Africa, a scholar-
ship fund, and interventions with B.C. school districts found to
be using racially biased materials. In the late 1950s and early 1960s,
for example, a Grade 4 workbook titled "Ten Little Niggers" was
being used in B.C. classrooms, along with a book called "Uncle
Rufus" which fostered stereotyped images of Black people. The
BCAACP was not always successful in opposing use of such "learning materials," but it did call attention to the problem.

Investigating racist incidents has never been a major activity of
the Association—it has lacked the staff to do so—but it has been
involved in a number of such cases. Though each incident appeared
isolated, and was soon forgotten by most British Columbians, the
cases formed a familiar North American pattern. In 1959, the
Hudson's Bay Company was advertising sweaters in a shade called
"nigger brown." In 1960, a Vancouver motel refused to rent to
Blacks. In 1962, harassment of Blacks by immigration officials at
the border became a serious problem. A "Black Sambo Pancake

House" was opened in Vancouver in 1964. And throughout the early 1960s, well known business firms in the Lower Mainland refused to hire Blacks. The BCAACP succeeded in fighting some of these cases, but not all: the HBC changed its advertising, and the pancake house changed its name, but "Ten Little Niggers" stayed in the schools and the motel's policy was upheld in court.

In the 1970s, B.C. Blacks made progress, but slowly. Vancouver's first Black policeman joined the force in 1970; his colleagues continued to harass Blacks on the street, including a lawyer and an internationally famous entertainer. The BCAACP won battles against housing discrimination, but Black students at Simon Fraser University were still coping with suspicious border officials in 1972. Even in the late 1970s, Blacks visiting Canada from the U.S. or the West Indies continued to encounter problems at the border.

Nevertheless, B.C. Blacks in the 1970s found white attitudes growing more positive—sometimes for ironic reasons. Canadians' exposure to American mass media has shown them new images of Blacks as sharp-witted, decisive, tough, and elegant, though it is doubtful whether Shaft is less of a stereotype than was Stepin Fetchit. Canadian whites, especially young people, have tended to accept this new image as uncritically as their grandparents accepted the comic "darkies" in *Maclean's* stories of the 1920s. As a result, a 1976 survey of racial attitudes in Lower Mainland schools found that white students generally considered it "cool" to be Black—though the same students were openly biased against East Indians, who were more numerous and less favored by the media.

The nature and numbers of B.C.'s modern Black community are difficult to determine. In 1971, the BCAACP conducted a survey which, though incomplete and now somewhat out-of-date, described the community in more detail than ever before; its findings can be cautiously extrapolated to the late 1970s. The survey made an "educated guess" at a Black population of between two and three thousand, but this figure is almost certainly too low: in 1958, the census counted 2,800 in Vancouver alone. Assuming typical Canadian birthrates and even modest immigration since then, the late-1970s total is probably near 10,000—a figure considered conservative by a Vancouver official in the Citizenship Branch of the Department of the Secretary of State. Most of these live in the Lower Mainland and Victoria, but the 1971 survey found

Blacks living all over the province, from the Peace River to the Kootenays and from Prince Rupert to the west coast of Vancouver Island.

Of those surveyed, 53 percent were Canadian-born and 22 percent were natives of British Columbia. Despite the relatively large Black populations in Ontario and the Maritimes, immigrants from those provinces formed just 4 percent of those surveyed; Alberta-born Blacks made up 14 percent. Of those from outside Canada, 29 percent were from the U.S., 13 percent from the West Indies (a figure the survey suggested was too low to be accurate), and 5 percent from Africa.

Given these diverse backgrounds, the survey did not examine the educational levels of adult Blacks. It did find that Black children's school enrolment was that of a fairly young community: out of a total of 148 children, 104 were in preschool or elementary programs, 35 were in secondary schools, 1 in vocational training, and 8 in colleges, universities, or other post-secondary programs. If the sample surveyed was typical of the whole population, then B.C. colleges and universities will enrol sizable numbers of Blacks in the 1980s.

As in the pioneer period, British Columbia's Blacks have pursued urban middle-class occupations. The survey found that 40 percent of those interviewed were white-collar workers, semiprofessionals, and professionals; 17 percent were skilled workers; 26 percent were semiskilled and 16 percent unskilled. Perhaps because such fields as teaching and social work opened to Blacks relatively early, they were, by the late 1970s, employed in "social service" professions out of all proportion to their numbers, but were relatively rare in medicine and the law; even so, Val Romilly is a prominent lawyer in Smithers, and his brother Selwyn is a Provincial Court Judge in Terrace.

Those conducting the 1971 survey felt that the Black community was "very weak in the areas of business, the white collar world, which in most communities supplies the economic power and the political aspirants." Perhaps so, but Black enterprises are energetically promoted by Sepia 30, an organization of Black businessmen in Vancouver. And the social service professions have provided a good source of political aspirants, including MLAs Rosemary

Brown and Emery Barnes and former North Vancouver alderman John Braithwaite.

The survey found that Blacks, like most Canadians, tend to have relatively small families: most had two or three children, though a few had as many as five or six. About 30 percent of the marriages were interracial. Sixty percent of those surveyed were married, 26 percent were single, and 14 percent were separated or divorced.

Vancouver's Blacks, as one would expect in a relatively young and mobile population, have established no clear pattern in their choice of housing. Most of those surveyed in 1971 lived in the city itself or in adjacent Burnaby, with a scattering on the North Shore and in the southern suburbs of Richmond, Delta, and Surrey. Most had lived in their present residence fewer than five years. Half owned their own homes, usually a single-family dwelling; 90 percent expressed satisfaction with the area they lived in. Of those renting, 31 percent said they had encountered some discrimination in housing, or had avoided potential problems; this clearly indicates a continuing and serious problem.

Discrimination, actual or potential, is in a way more difficult for B.C. Blacks than for Americans precisely because it is relatively rare and affects such a small number of people. Those who suffer because of racist acts or attitudes have few resources to combat it; the larger white community is either ignorant of their problem or prefers to think that the problem does not exist at all. British Columbia's Blacks might therefore be compared to a population long isolated from a particular disease and consequently very vulnerable when the disease does strike. Bill Long, an instructor at Douglas College, discovered this in 1976 when he began to receive threatening phone calls. His persecutor tried to get him fired from his job and once even attempted to kidnap Long's son from school. These incidents culminated in 1977 with the burning of Long's car. Long finally went to the media; he told an interviewer that he had never been subjected to such harassment even as a civil-rights worker in the American South in the 1960s.

Such a campaign merited, and got, widespread publicity which reminded all British Columbians that their province might well harbor racists. Publicity is less readily given for the many Black individuals and groups who continue to enrich life in British Columbia. In addition to the BCAACP, other groups have worked to foster specific or general Black concerns. The Victoria Black People's Society, founded in the 1970s, has begun to draw together the 300 or more Blacks living in Victoria, its suburbs, and the Gulf Islands. The Jamaican-Caribbean Association has kept West Indian Blacks in touch with one another, as has the Caribe Club.

Perhaps one of the surest signs of the strength of the modern Black community has been its increasing cultural activity. Since the mid 1970s, Ernie King's Sepia Players have staged creditable productions of such works as *Boesman and Lena* and *Ceremonies in Dark Old Men*. Jenny LeGon's Troupe One has provided opportunities for young people to develop their abilities in dance; the Black Cultural Awareness Program, started in 1975 by Jay Burns, has helped introduce Black children to African and Caribbean dance and music, jazz, and Black cultural history. Probably the single most prominent Black artist in B.C. is Leon Bibb, an American-born singer who settled in Vancouver in the early 1970s. His performances in *Jacques Brel is Alive and Well and Living in Paris, Berlin to Broadway*, and numerous solo concerts have enhanced his already solid international reputation.

Surprisingly, almost no B.C. Blacks have portrayed their experience in fiction except for Truman Green. His short novel *A Credit to Your Race*, privately printed in early 1970s, describes a Black teenager's unhappy affair with a white girl. Though its plot is melodramatic, the story is convincing where it depicts an uncomprehending white society: a Surrey schoolteacher, for example, asks the protagonist's sister if she can "speak Negro." In his portrait of an uncertain, isolated young man trying to find a relationship with a society that would rather ignore him, Green has expressed the general status of the Black community in modern British Columbia. The biased and ignorant whites who fail to understand the protagonist are no mere stereotypes: in 1977, the school boards of Langley and Surrey prohibited classroom use of a slide-tape presentation on racism in B.C. history, ostensibly on the grounds that it was negative and might actually incite racism in students exposed to it.

Nowhere in the province are Blacks numerous enough — or united enough — to influence politics as the pioneers did. But in the

1970s, three Black politicians have won strong, repeated support at the polls despite what might seem impossible "handicaps." Not only are they all members of a very small racial minority, they are all from outside B.C. and two of them are naturalized Canadians. All are social workers strongly concerned with human problems in a province largely apathetic towards such problems. But John Braithwaite topped the polls when he first ran for alderman in North Vancouver City, and Emery Barnes and Rosemary Brown were among the few New Democratic MLAs who survived the Social Credit landslide in the provincial election of 1975.

Braithwaite, born in Ontario in 1929, gained his B.A. and M.S.W. at the University of Toronto. In 1956 he moved to B.C. and began work at North Shore Neighbourhood House; a year later, at 27, he became its executive director. In the following 20 years he saw the membership of NSNH rise from 200 to 1,000, and led a long campaign to faise funds for new facilities. A varsity basketball player at the University of Toronto, Braithwaite organized and coached the "Harlem Nocturnes," an all-Black team that won the B.C. provincial championship. Active in municipal politics by the nature of his job, Braithwaite often worked with the city council and with ratepayers' groups; these activities led to his first running for office in 1972. For the next four years, he was a conscientious, hard-working, and highly popular alderman. Though he left politics in 1976, some North Shore observers are convinced he could easily be elected mayor.

Emery Barnes, born in New Orleans, Louisiana in 1929, has succeeded in three careers. A member of the 1952 U.S. Olympic team, he won recognition as a high jumper; later he entered professional football, playing five years with the B.C. Lions. In his second career, as a social worker, he was director of children's and teenagers' programs at Gordon Neighbourhood House in Vancouver's West End; Director of Grandview Community Centre; Supervisor of Social Training at Haney Correctional Institute, and group worker at the Narcotic Addiction Foundation. Since 1972 he has been an MLA representing Vancouver Centre, serving as party whip during the NDP's years in power and as highways and public works critic in opposition.

Rosemary Brown immigrated to Canada from Jamaica in 1950. She holds degrees from McGill and the University of British Col-

umbia; during her career as a social worker she worked with the
Montreal Children's Hospital, the Children's Aid Society of B.C.,
and the Vancouver Neurological Society. In addition to her long-
standing membership in the BCAACP, she has been an active
feminist, serving as ombudswoman of the B.C. Status of Women
Council from 1970 to 1972 and as an articulate leader of the women's rights groups within the NDP. Elected as MLA for Vancouver-
Burrard in 1972, she served in the Barrett government on many
committees, including Health, Education and Human Resources;
Labour and Justice, and Municipal Affairs. She received the
United Nations Human Rights Fellowship in 1972, and the National
Black Award of Canada in 1973. In 1975 she ran a strong cam-
paign for the leadership of the federal NDP, coming in second to
acting leader Ed Broadbent.

This background, however, was not enough to establish Brown's
credentials as a Canadian for at least one of her fellow-citizens.
During a debate in the B.C. legislature in 1977, Social Credit
MLA Pat Jordan interrupted Brown to ask: "Why doesn't the
member go back to Jamaica?" This provoked cries of "Shame"
and "Withdraw" from other New Democrats; Jordan explained
herself. "I only asked if the member is so concerned with problems
in the developing countries, why doesn't she go back to her own
country?"

"The member is operating under misinformation," Brown
replied. "This is my country."

Jordan withdrew her remarks, but only after being asked to do
so three times. Next day the Vancouver *Sun* commented on the
episode in a brief editorial titled "Hick": "Much as we'd like to tell
Pat Jordan to go back where she came from, it's perfectly obvious
that she never left." And Lisa Hobbs, associate editor of the *Sun,*
observed in a long article condemning Jordan's remarks that "the
very thing we need to keep the show on the road is *more* citizens
who are as strong, intelligent, and involved in their community as
is Rosemary Brown. The value of her contribution to the province's
political and social consciousness is already beyond dispute."

Black contributions to political life have also included strong
grassroots support to all political parties and to various community-
action groups. Given this involvement in the larger society, it
seems extremely unlikely that they could ever be subjected to the

kind of mass persecution once endured by British Columbia's Japanese and Chinese communities. They have therefore had an opportunity to build their own community positively, with few of the disadvantages besetting the Blacks of the United States. However, their dispersion and the lack of a perceived threat have not helped them to unite; like Canada itself, British Columbia's Black community is not a spontaneous, "natural" entity but one created and sustained by the will of its members. As in the province's pioneer days, modern Blacks are individualists who prefer like Arthur Clore to "stand on their own two feet." And like the pioneers, they are torn between the desire to pursue their own lives and the awareness that—like it or not—they are part of a great world people whose hopes and sorrows cannot be ignored.

The British historian A.J.P. Taylor has asserted that "we learn nothing from history but the infinite variety of men's behaviour." But no one familiar with British Columbia could fail to see a depressing lack of variety in its history: one generation after another has confronted squalor amid wealth, political corruption and incompetence, demagoguery, and racial oppression. In our own time, racism is nearly as strong as it was in the 1860s, though far less publicly acceptable. Its modern apologists dare not echo Matthew Macfie's fears of "mongrelization"; they prefer to argue that nonwhites are unable to assimilate into the larger society. In fact, every nonwhite immigrant group in B.C. has suffered precisely because it *has* assimilated. In a competitive, free-enterprise society, Blacks and Asians have been competitive and enterprising indeed, and their resulting prosperity has irritated those whites unwilling or unable to play the game so strenuously. In the 1860s the Blacks were the chief target; late in the century it was the turn of the Chinese; in the early 1900s, that of the East Indians and Japanese. In the 1970s, East Indians of African origin have recapitulated the Black pioneers' experience. Successful but unpopular in Uganda, Kenya, Zaire and other countries, many have sought a refuge from oppression in Canada. Their energy and entrepreneurial skills have enabled them to prosper, yet they have encountered resentment and distrust from the society they are helping to enrich.

If Taylor is wrong, and something can be learned from our history, it is that British Columbians have always demonstrated their wealth by wasting it — especially their human wealth. The Indians took slaves for show, not for work; the white pioneers despised the contributions of Blacks and Orientals, and did their best to discourage them from settling permanently. Fortunately for their own best interests, the whites did not succeed, but they did manage to keep more Blacks from coming north. Had Black migration continued (as it surely would have if Douglas's original promises had been kept), modern B.C. might well have experienced some of the racial tensions of the U.S., but it would also have become a livelier, more complex, and less self-deceiving society. By failing to live up to their professions of equality and fair treatment for all, the white pioneers of B.C. deprived their descendants of an immense human resource. Now, as new groups come seeking the same equality the Black pioneers sought, modern British Columbians can withhold it and impoverish themselves, or give it — and enrich themselves beyond the dreams of the pioneers.

When asked why he had come to Canada, Arthur Clore replied: "There is hope in this country. Yes, that is what has kept me here — the difference between hope and no hope." The old prospector chose his words well. There is hope in this country, but the achievement of genuine racial equality is yet to come.

BIBLIOGRAPHY

Most of the material in this book was drawn from the following published sources, as well as contemporary newspaper stories too numerous to mention. Those interested in consulting such sources will find the catalogues of the British Columbia Provincial Archives a convenient access. James Pilton's thesis provides many references to relevant news stories and other documents; some very useful material was also supplied through interviews and correspondence with persons mentioned in the introduction.

Among the newspapers of the pioneer period, the following were read in whole or in part: *The British Colonist* (Victoria); *The British Columbian* (New Westminster); *The Cariboo Sentinel* (Barkerville); *The Elevator* (San Francisco); *The Times* (New Westminster); *The Daily Evening Bulletin* (San Francisco); *The Gazette* (Victoria). The modern *Sun* and *Province* of Vancouver, and the *Colonist* of Victoria, provide a number of stories on the subject, not all of them reliable.

Brief comments follow some references.

Akrigg, George P.V. and Helen B. Akrigg. *British Columbia chronicle, 1778-1846: adventures by sea and land.* Vancouver: Discovery Press, 1975. Useful background information on the discovery and development of the Pacific Northwest.

_____. *British Columbia chronicle, 1847-1871: gold & colonists.* Vancouver: Discovery Press, 1977. A good general survey, but contains little on the role of the Blacks in the colonial period.

Anonymous. "Biographical and Historical Memoirs of Pulaski [and other counties], Arkansas." Chicago: Goodspeed, 1889. Biographical material on Mifflin Gibbs.

Anonymous. "Car burned in race-hate campaign." *Sun,* March 25, 1977. Describes harassment of a black family in modern Vancouver.

Anonymous. "Colored man was a judge." Little Rock *Gazette,* August 24, 1903. Interview with Mifflin Gibbs.

Anonymous. "Henry McDame — Black Prospector." *Canada West Magazine,* vol. 5, no. 4 (Fall 1975), pp. 31-37. The only modern account of this man; throws light on Black miners other than McDame as well.

Anonymous. "Mifflin W. Gibbs called by death." Little Rock *Gazette,* July 12, 1915.

Asante, Nadine. *The history of Terrace.* Terrace: Terrace Public Library Association, 1972. Material on Arthur Clore.

————. "Our Negroes: the fewer the safer." *Sun,* August 28, 1965.

Balf, Mary. *Kamloops: a history of the district up to 1914.* Kamloops: History Committee, Kamloops Museum, 1969. Useful material on John Freemont Smith.

Bancroft, Hubert Howe. *History of the northwest coast* (2 vols.). New York: Bancroft, 1884.

————. *History of the Pacific states, vol. 27: British Columbia.* San Francisco: The History Company, 1887.

Baxter, Betty. "Jim Anderson...Gulf Islands' old-timer and friend of the children." *Province,* January 1, 1946. Some useful information, but patronizing in tone.

Beasley, Delilah L. *The Negro trail blazers of California.* Los Angeles, 1919. Material on Mifflin Gibbs.

Begbie, Matthew Baillie. "Notes of evidence & memorandum to accompany notes--Ra. vs. Barry for the murder of Blessing at Richfield, 1 July 1867." Victoria: Provincial Archives. The major source for the Blessing murder and Wellington Moses' role in Barry's conviction.

Bowes, Gordon E., ed. *Peace River chronicles.* Vancouver: Prescott Publishing, 1963. Includes material on Daniel Williams.

British Columbia Association for the Advancement of Colored People. *Black community survey.* Unpublished report, 1971.

Brown, Rosemary. "Negroes." In Norris, John, ed., *Strangers entertained: a history of the ethnic groups of British Columbia.* Vancouver: British Columbia Centennial '71 Committee, 1971. A good short survey of Blacks in B.C. since 1858.

Bruce, Marian. "Former slave's story tells of island's early days." *Sun,* May 6, 1974. About the Stark family.

Campbell, Aileen. "Born a slave, Mathilda nears 104." *Province,* January 29, 1963. Profile of Mathilda Boynton, a well-known figure in Vancouver's modern Black community.

Clark, Cecil. "Nugget tiepin was murder clue." *Colonist,* May 30, 1965. The Blessing murder.

————. *Tales of the B.C. provincial police.* Sidney, B.C.: Gray's Publishing, 1971.

Colman, Mary Elizabeth. "'English Bay Joe' was our first life guard." *Sun,* August 23, 1961. Feature on Joe Fortes.

Cornwallis, Kinahan. *The new El Dorado; or, British Columbia.* London: Newby, 1858. One or two anti-Black anecdotes from the first days of the gold rush; mentions Black constables.

Cracroft, Sophia. *Lady Franklin visits the Pacific Northwest.* Edited by Dorothy Blakey Smith. Victoria: Provincial Archives, 1974. Much useful material on Blacks in Victoria, including Gibbs, Moses, Charles Mitchell, and members of the African Rifles.

Davis, Chuck, ed. *The Vancouver book.* Vancouver: J.J. Douglas, 1976. Some mention of Vancouver's Black community in the early twentieth century.

Downs, Art. *Wagon road north: the story of the Cariboo gold rush in historical photos.* Quesnel: Northwest Digest, 1960.

Duff, Wilson. *The Indian history of B.C., vol. I: The impact of the white man.* (2d ed.) Victoria: Provincial Museum of Natural History and Anthropology, 1969. Valuable insights into Indian-colonist relationships and the effect of the 1862 smallpox epidemic.

Eberts, Tony. "This was freedom." *Province,* January 4, 1958. The Stark family.

Fawcett, Edgar. *Some reminiscences of old Victoria.* Toronto: William Briggs, 1912.

Flucke, A.F. "Early days on Salt Spring Island." *British Columbia Historical Quarterly,* vol. 15 (1951), pp. 161-199.

Foner, Philip S. "The colored inhabitants of Vancouver Island." *B.C. Studies,* no. 8 (Winter 1970-71), pp. 29-33. Reprints an anonymous Black's impression of Victoria in the mid-1860s.

Genini, Ronald. "The Fraser-Cariboo gold rushes: comparisons and contrasts with the California gold rush." *Journal of the West,* vol. 11 no. 3 (July 1972), pp. 470-487.

Gibbs, Mifflin Wistar. *Shadow and light: an autobiography.* Washington, D.C., 1902. Facsimile edition published New York: Arno Press & The New York Times, 1968. A key document, as interesting for what Gibbs omits as for what he includes. He says very little about his personal life, his family, and his struggles with racism in Victoria, but he gives us vivid descriptions of mining in the Queen Charlottes and the atmosphere in San Francisco before the Black emigration to the British Northwest.

Glover, George H. *History of the United Church of Canada, north and south Saanich areas.* Pamphlet, n.p., 1957. Biographical material on the Alexander family.

Gould, Jan. *Women of British Columbia.* Saanichton: Hancock House, 1975. A good account of Sylvia Stark; includes material on her daughter Emma.

Green, Truman. *A credit to your race.* Tsawwassen: Simple Thoughts Press, n.d. Short novel about a Black youth growing up in Surrey.

Gregson, Harry. *A history of Victoria 1842-1970.* Victoria: Victoria Observer Publishing, 1970.

Hamilton, Bea. *Salt Spring Island.* Vancouver: Mitchell Press, 1969. Includes a lively but seriously inaccurate account of the early Black settlers on the island.

Hannaford, Nigel E. "The Death of Nigger Dan." *Canada West Magazine,* vol. 6, no. 3 (Summer 1976), pp. 13-15. Presents a somewhat negative account of Daniel Williams.

Heilbron, William C. "Piracy—English Bay Version." *Province,* February 11, 1961. Personal reminiscence of Joe Fortes.

Helmcken, John Sebastian. *The reminiscences of Doctor John Sebastian Helmcken,* edited by Dorothy Blakey Smith. Vancouver: University of British Columbia Press, 1975.

Higgins, D.W. *The mystic spring and other tales of western life.* Toronto:

William Briggs, 1904. Somewhat romanticized anecdotes of colonial days.

_____. *The passing of a race.* Toronto: William Briggs, 1905.

Hope, Grace. "The passing of Old Black Joe." *Province,* August 12, 1928. Describes the burning of Joe Fortes's old cottage.

Howay, F.W. *British Columbia: the making of a province.* Toronto: Ryerson, 1928.

_____. "The Negro immigration into Vancouver Island in 1858." *British Columbia Historical Quarterly,* vol. 3 (1939), pp. 101-113. One of the earliest serious studies of the subject.

Hutchinson, Bruce. *The Fraser.* Toronto: Clarke, Irwin, 1950.

Irby, Charles C. "Black settlers on Salt Spring Island in the nineteenth century." *Association of Pacific Coast Geographers 1974 Yearbook,* pp. 35-44. Corvallis: Oregon State University Press, 1974.

Johnson, F. Henry. *John Jessop: goldseeker and educator.* Vancouver: Mitchell Press, 1971. Contains material on John C. Jones's teaching career.

La Terreur, Marc, ed. *Dictionary of Canadian Biography,* vol. 10 (1871-1880). Toronto: University of Toronto Press, 1966. Material on John Sullivan Deas.

Lawrance, Scott. "The Haida potato." In White, Howard, ed., *Raincoast Chronicles First Five,* p. 50. Madeira Park: Harbour Publishing, 1976. Suggests Haidas obtained the potato from Japan, before whites' arrival in the Northwest.

Lopez, Sandra. *BCAACP summer project 1976: a report of the history of the association from 1958-1975.* Unpublished report, 1976.

Lovell's Gazetteer of British North America, 1873.

Luckingham, Bradford. "Immigrant life in emergent San Francisco." *Journal of the West,* vol. 12 no. 4 (October 1973), pp. 600-617. Useful background on San Francisco's Black community in the 1850s.

Lozovsky, Nora N. "A directory of ethno-cultural organizations in British Columbia." Vancouver: Department of the Secretary of State, 1975.

MacEwan, Grant. *John Ware's cattle country.* Edmonton: Institute of Applied Art, 1960. Biography of a well-known Black Alberta rancher.

Macfie, Matthew. *Vancouver Island and British Columbia. Their history, resources and prospects.* London: Longman, 1865. Facsimile edition published Toronto: Coles Publishing, 1972. A key document, offering insights into the racial attitudes and anxieties of many white colonists.

MacGregor, James G. *The land of Twelve Foot Davis: a history of the Peace River country.* Edmonton: Applied Arts Products, 1952. Gives a fairer account of Daniel Williams than do most sources.

Mayne, Richard Charles. *Four years in British Columbia and Vancouver Island.* London: John Murray, 1862. Fascimile edition published New York: Johnson Reprint, 1969. A British naval officer's experiences in the Northwest, with some comments on the Black community in Victoria.

Meany, Edward S. *Vancouver's discovery of Puget Sound.* New York: Macmillan, 1907. Facsimile edition published Portland: Binfords & Mart, 1957.

Morley, Alan. *Vancouver: from milltown to metropolis* (2d ed.). Vancouver: Mitchell Press, 1969. Some material on Joe Fortes and on the Black woman involved in the Chinatown riots of 1907.

————. "Vancouver loved Joe Fortes, and he repaid the love in full." *Province,* September 10, 1955.

Morton, James W. *In the sea of sterile mountains: the Chinese in British Columbia.* Vancouver: J.J.Douglas, 1974. An excellent history of the Chinese community; some mention of the Blacks, especially Willis Bond.

Moses, Wellington Delany. *Diaries.* Victoria: Provincial Archives.

Nesbitt, James K. "Christmas dinner for 50 cents." *Colonist,* December 23, 1962. Mentions the Alexanders' golden wedding anniversary.

————."History neglects famous Ringo." *Colonist,* October 8, 1961. Quotes extensively from an 1880s account of Sam Ringo and his restaurant.

————."Hot time in the old town." *Colonist,* April 26, 1959. Describes a brawl between Black and white teamsters.

————. "Old homes and families." *Colonist,* January 31, 1954. Willis Bond's speeches and scrapes with the law.

Nichols, Robert H. "Mystery of the old hut." *Sun,* January 16, 1954. Dubious anecdotes about Blacks on Saltspring Island.

Nicholson, George. "They were the first." *Colonist,* May 21, 1961. A slightly inaccurate account of the African Rifles.

Nicholson, Ian. "Joe Fortes — little children loved him." *Province,* July 19, 1947.

Nicol, Eric. *Vancouver.* Toronto: Doubleday Canada, 1970.

Norcross, Elizabeth Blanche. *The warm land.* Duncan: E.B. Norcross, 1959. Lists "Lewis" Stark among early settlers on Vancouver Island.

Ormsby, Margaret. *British Columbia: a history.* Toronto: Macmillan, 1971. This standard history makes little mention of the Blacks, and is patronizing when it does.

Pethick, Derek. *James Douglas: servant of two empires.* Vancouver: Mitchell Press, 1969.

_____.*Men of British Columbia.* Saanichton: Hancock House, 1975. Considerable attention to Mifflin Gibbs and a few other Blacks.

_____.*Victoria: the fort.* Vancouver: Mitchell Press, 1968. A good account of the gold-rush period.

Pilton, James W. "Negro settlement in B.C., 1858-1871." Unpublished M.A. thesis, University of British Columbia, 1951. The major source on the Black pioneers, and an invaluable guide to contemporary documents about them. While Pilton sometimes accepts white opinions about the Blacks too uncritically, most of his conclusions stand up very well after a quarter of a century.

Pires, Ben J. "Saltspring: a sense of freedom." *Beautiful B.C.,* Summer 1975, pp. 38-44.

Ralston, H. Keith. "John Sullivan Deas: a Black entrepreneur in British Columbia salmon canning." *B.C. Studies,* no. 32 (Winter 1976-77) pp. 64-78. A very useful study of a little-known Black pioneer.

Ramsey, Bruce. *Barkerville: a guide to the fabulous Cariboo gold camp* (2d ed.). Vancouver: Mitchell Press, 1961. Mentions several Blacks.

_____."Remembering the days of 'Old Black Joe.'" *Province,* March 16, 1964.

Reid, J.H. Stewart. *Mountains, men and rivers.* New York: Bouregy & Curl. 1954. Good account of "Ned McGowan's War."

Reid, P.H. "Segregation in British Columbia." *The Bulletin,* United Church of Canada, vol. 16 (1963), pp. 1-15. The major source on the church dispute between Clarke and Macfie.

Reid, Robie L. "How one slave became free." *British Columbia Historical Quarterly,* vol. 6 (1942), pp. 251-256. When not trying to be witty, Reid provides some useful information on the Charles Mitchell case and the legal position taken by Attorney-General Cary in the case.

Roberts, Eric. *Salt Spring Saga.* Ganges: Driftwood Publishing, 1962. Probably the most reliable account of pioneer days on Saltspring, with considerable mention of the Blacks.

St. Pierre, Paul. "Freedom built Negro colony; Yankee dollar pulled it down." *Sun,* April 6, 1960. Interview with Mrs. Myrtle Holloman, granddaughter of Sylvia Stark.

Sage, Walter N. *Sir James Douglas and British Columbia.* Toronto: University of Toronto Press, 1930.

Scholefield, E.O.S. and F.W. Howay. *British Columbia, from the earliest times to the present.* Vancouver: S.J. Clarke, 1914.

Sharp, Brenda G. "Murder followed the Starks." *Colonist,* October 27, 1963.

Shelton, George W., ed. *British Columbia and confederation.* Victoria: Morriss Printing, 1967.

Smith, Dorothy Blakey. *James Douglas: father of British Columbia.* Toronto: Oxford University Press, 1971.

Stanley, Gerald. "The politics of the antebellum far west: the impact of the slavery and race issues in California." *Journal of the West,* vol. 16, no. 4 (October 1977), pp. 19-25. While not mentioning the Black emigration, this article makes clear the pervasiveness of anti-Black sentiment in California during the 1850s.

Tulloch, Headley. *Black Canadians: a long line of fighters.* Toronto: NC Press, 1975. Concentrates on Blacks in eastern Canada, but has some mention of those in British Columbia.

Virgin, Victor E. *History of the north and south Saanich pioneers and district.* Victoria: Saanich Pioneer Society, n.d. Mentions several Black families in addition to the Alexanders.

Waddington, Alfred. *The Fraser mines vindicated, or the history of four months.* Victoria, 1858. The first book published in Victoria, and a vivid account of the impact of the gold rush.

Walden, Frederick Ellsworth. "The social history of Victoria, British Columbia." Unpublished B.A. essay, University of British Columbia, 1951.

Wallace, Marie Stark. "Notes made by Maria Albertina Stark (afterwards Mrs. Wallace) from the recollections of her mother, Sylvia Stark, who was born a slave in Clay County, Missouri, and settled on Salt Spring Island with her husband, Louis Stark, and family in the year 1860, as homesteaders." Victoria: Provincial Archives. A remarkable and important document which, despite some minor inaccuracies, offers dramatic and detailed descriptions of pioneer life on Saltspring Island.

Wild, Roland. *Amor De Cosmos.* Toronto: Ryerson Press, 1958.

[Wilson, E.F.] *Salt Spring Island, B.C.* Victoria: Colonist Press, 1895. Some mention of Blacks living on the island at the end of the century.

Winks, Robin W. *The Blacks in Canada: a history.* Montreal: McGill-Queen's University Press and New Haven: Yale University Press, 1971. Contains a great deal of information and helps to place the experience of B.C.'s Blacks in the larger Canadian context. Some minor inaccuracies.

_____.*Canada and the United States: the civil war years.* Baltimore: Johns Hopkins Press, 1962.

Wood, Anne. "B.C.'s colored colony." *Province,* June 29, 1935. Interview with Fielding William Spotts.

Woodcock, George. *Amor De Cosmos: journalist and reformer.* Toronto: Oxford University Press, 1975.

INDEX